Real, Not Perfect

How to Become Your Happy, Authentic Self

Real, Not Perfect

How to Become Your Happy, Authentic Self

Holly Raychelle Hughes

Table of Contents

One

Introduction

Let me introduce myself. My name is Holly Hughes, and I am an intuitive, an author, and a public speaker, along with being a daughter, wife, friend, and mother. I love dancing, Halloween, and being outside. Other times, I like solitude and quiet. I'm so many things, but I know what you really want to know. After all, knowing things is one of my gifts.

I'm often asked to define my intuition and explain how I know what I can't possibly know and how I do what I do. There is no single answer to this question any more than there is a one-word answer as to who I am.

Let's start by creating a shared language. I'll do my best to address the most common questions with my definitions of the intuitive gifts I possess.

Let's do it Q&A style. Consider the following questions that have been posed to me by clients and readers. Please keep in mind that these are *my* definitions of my gifts. Others may use different terminology.

What is an intuitive?

An intuitive person is one who can connect with the spiritual realm.

What does that mean?

It means I feel things past the five senses of sight, hearing, taste, touch, and smell.

The best way I know how to explain this extra sensory part is by asking if you've ever walked into a room after people were arguing and felt uneasy? I feel similar sensations all the time. My intuition allows me to connect to things which the human eye cannot see and/or understand. I connect to sources of love and light, including spirit guides, light beings, angels, and a host of other ascended souls.

How does Holly know the names, types of beings, and energy she sees and feels?

The guides who come to offer healing energy and support tell me their names and place images of themselves in my mind's eye. The guides are not limited to any religious background or dogma. A loving presence does not discriminate because of religious or spiritual beliefs.

Are there different types of intuitives?

Yes! Some people can tap into different energies and vibrations to receive additional information.

I work a bit differently than other intuitives I've met, but it's always fun and encouraging to receive the same messages as another person. The validation leads me further along the path of being a healer.

There are five abilities most people ask about; they are called the Clairs. These are my definitions of how I experience them:

Clairvoyance: This ability gets lots of press and screen time. It's the ability to see images with or without your eyes. Think of seeing visions in your mind, like dreams while you are awake. It includes seeing spirits, guides, angels, dark energy, and auras.

Clairaudience: This ability allows you to hear things in your mind even though there isn't someone physically present with you.

Clairsentience: This is the ability to sense things in your body that aren't your aches, pains, illnesses, joys, or muscle memories. It's the body's ability to mirror what is happening in another person's body.

Claircognizance: This is the hardest of the Clairs to explain. It's the ability to suddenly know something to be true even though there is no way you could know it. It's like having all of the answers for a test you didn't study for, yet you still earn a perfect score. You just know it.

Clairgustance: This is the ability to taste items that aren't in your mouth.

How is an empath different than a clairsentient person?

To me, an empath is a person who takes the clairsentient gift to the next level. An empath senses, internalizes, and experiences other people's emotions. An empath feels the other person so acutely they may have difficulty discerning and assigning whether the emotion belongs to them or someone else. An empath is another person's emotionally identical twin. In comparison, a clairsentient person is looking for and recognizing an emotional truth.

What abilities does Holly have?

I'm lucky enough to have all of these abilities. They are my normal. And I use all of them when I work with

3

clients. I also have the ability to move the energy in and around a person's body.

Still have questions about being an intuitive and how it works?

I have thought about this a lot. How can I explain how my gifts work while maintaining clients' privacy? Because the easiest way to demonstrate how I work and explain how I'm wired is to share success stories. However, since my room is a safe space, I won't break client confidentiality and trust. Instead, I'll share a few examples of people and their concerns as general examples.

I share my healing journey when working with clients. It's my way of saying, "I have made mistakes in my life and survived things that devastated me. And no matter how many painful experiences I've had, I have done the healing work and felt better."

It's impossible to answer every question about how I utilize my intuitive gifts. I'm asking you to take a leap of faith and trust me, as my clients do. Know that as you go through this book, I'll delve deeper into intuitive healing, and your understanding will increase.

You don't have to know how I work for the healing to happen. Isn't that beautiful? I have no idea how electricity turns on my lights, but I trust that when I flip a switch, the light will come on, and I'll be able to see more clearly.

How can Holly help you?

The most miraculous thing about how I use the incredible gifts with which I have been blessed is that I'm able to cut through all the bullshit and get to the heart of a client's issue. When we have a session together, you don't have to dig up your past or tell me your family history. All you have to do is start talking about what's bothering you, and I will sense, feel, and experience the rest. It's during the sensory experience that I begin to see and hear your guides.

If you're still not sure what that means, think of it like this: You have a "radio" frequency, and I turn the dial and connect to you. Then I use all of the tools in my intuitive toolbox to help you move past the pain, shame, guilt, thought process, emotional stories, and past to guide you in creating your future.

Since I can see and move energy, I can help you to free yourself from the emotional weight you carry. The easiest way to describe this is to think about when a dryer sheet is stuck to your clothes, but you can't see it. Soon, someone takes it off for you. Think of that dryer sheet as bad energy, and I'm the person removing it for you, just as I am helping you to remove what you can't see.

For those of you who know about the energy centers of the body, including chakras and auric fields, I have the ability to heal them.

What if I'm embarrassed to share what's going on in my life?

My office is a judgment-free zone. Shame and guilt are emotions I help you process and move through by navigating your past and experiences, along with every other element holding you back from your ability to thrive.

My abilities are your connection to the supernatural in your life that you can't feel, since there are those who haven't experienced intuitive healing or people with extrasensory abilities before. My specialty is helping people through transition points in their lives.

HOLLY R. HUGHES

If you are willing to change, I can receive and relate the messages needed to support you. I can guarantee that, as you read, you'll:

1. Believe I want to help you become your most authentic self.
2. Feel better and have hope.

You want to feel better, right? You want to let go of what no longer works for you and get on with living a happier life free of the shame, guilt, pain, embarrassment, and definitions of your past?

I'm going to help you do that. We'll start with the labels with which you define yourself and move through healing the hurt, releasing the past, and freeing you up to be the person you want to be. The real you. Your true, authentic self. The person who doesn't have to please others to be validated, appreciated, or loved.

Know that I was called to write this book. I knew you needed some help, and I answered the call on faith. I'm ready to support you through change. Are you willing to do the work?

When should you try intuitive healing?

People come to me when traditional therapy and advice from friends isn't helping. They need more than talk therapy. They're looking for a personal and spiritual connection, and they need empathy and understanding given to them with kindness — and with the promise of mystical assistance.

I'm an intuitive healer with over twenty years experience. My gifts help me get to the root of an issue when a person can't even name the problem. All they know is something is off, or they're unhappy or stuck, but they can't say why. My intuitive abilities let me see inside a person's body and see their infinite soul's magical colors. As an intuitive, I can cut to the chase of emotional issues and speak about the root cause, because that is the information the universal energy shares with me. I connect with clients on a spiritual and emotional level where words can't connect the dots, and where fear, or patterns of feeling less-than, can't get in the way. There is no judgment or agenda in my room; all I want is for people to heal and become authentically true to themselves. I want them to be happy being who they are.

What's a healing session with Holly like?

When a client first steps into my office, I receive immediate information about them through physical sensations in my body. I get aches and pains, numbness, gurgles in my stomach, and even sharp, needle-like headaches. I can sometimes taste things like memories, and it is usually a taste that evokes an emotional response in my clients, like tobacco or a favorite food. I see pictures and moments of what's going on with a person, and they play like movies in my mind. I see divine beings — call them what you feel most comfortable with, whether that is spirit guides, angels, highest self, Universal Masters, goddesses. I call them interdimensional beings because it encompasses all of the realms of possibilities and faiths. Sometimes I see family members who have passed.

Healing sessions are made up of two parts. The first part is where we talk. As we speak, I receive messages, and I relay them to you.

The second part is the energy work. This is when a client receives physical, spiritual, and mental healing. Your body also tells me things your mind does not, and

I often get a complete picture of the issues that need to be healed. I'm a conduit for divine healing.

Has Holly always had these gifts?

Seeing and feeling things other people didn't experience was something I never used to talk about. I honestly didn't realize most people didn't have these gifts. My abilities have always been there, but I didn't make a career of them. I used them to guide my decision-making process and as a party trick. However, my intuition grew stronger when I paid attention to it, so I studied how to control it. Truth be told, I didn't really like dead relatives of friends showing up to chat when I was enjoying myself with friends. I had to learn how to turn it off and on.

I didn't own my gifts and call myself an intuitive until after I recovered from a deep depression when I had lost my abilities. The world fell silent and dark around me. I thought, *Is this how everyone else feels?* I hated how silent the world became. Hearing, feeling, and seeing all of the wonderful things I do is my normal, and it had seemingly disappeared. I had to heal from my depression before my gifts returned. Then I began to know something I couldn't know, such as feeling how the person sitting near me was sad, or knowing the person behind me in the snack line at the movies was cheating. I could feel when dark energy was around me, because fear crept up my neck and I felt my senses fire up and tell me to get away.

Being intuitive doesn't mean I don't suffer the same heartaches and pains as most people. What it does mean is that I feel the support of divine beings that most people don't. I can see that there is more to this life than meets the eye. I know love continues, and there is good and bad in everything. I also know we are loved and supported, even when our senses don't feel it, and our hearts and minds don't believe it.

How does Holly experience her abilities?

I feel all kinds of vibrations all the time from people, places, and objects. I receive images from a person, which is like having multiple screens open on a computer. I can often see what a client is thinking or hear their thoughts. For example, once I kept seeing a yellow banana. I didn't understand what it had to do with anything, but it wouldn't go away, so I decided to risk looking stupid.

"I keep seeing a banana," I said to my client. "I don't know what it means, but I feel as if I have to tell you that. Does it mean something to you?"

The man sitting across from me started to laugh. "I told myself I'd know you were the real thing if you said ''banana.'"

"You were testing me?" I asked. It's important to know that I really don't like my clairvoyant abilities being tested.

"Yes," he said, without apology. After that moment, he became much more open to my healing abilities.

Most people don't come to me so they can test me. They come knowing something is not working for them in their lives, and they want the kind of help I offer.

Can you give me examples of what is involved in a healing session?

Here are a few examples of first sessions:

A girl named Shane arrived at my office early for her appointment. Her hair was neat, long, and styled, without a wisp out of place. It was golden brown, and I could tell from the care she took with it that it was one of her most valued physical traits. The multicolored scarf around her neck was tied in a French knot and didn't move when she moved. It was as if her exterior body was made of stone, and her clothes and jewelry were carved from the same marble, smooth and pristine. Her boots were clean, without one scuff mark. She smiled nervously at me as I welcomed her into my office.

When I met her eyes, all I felt in my body was heartbreak and stomach pain, as if someone she loved had died a horrible death, and she was being rejected and shunned by every person she knew. She sat, and I smiled, meeting her eyes, hoping to make her feel safe, because my intuition told me she didn't know the feeling of safety.

I asked if she'd ever seen an intuitive healer before, and she told me she hadn't. I explained what would happen during the next hour.

"We'll sit here and talk for about thirty or forty minutes. I will see, hear, and feel things about you during that time, and I'll share them with you. Then we'll move over to the massage table, where you'll keep all of your clothes on, and I will walk around you and hover my hands over your body, very similar to Reiki, but not Reiki, and I'll receive information from your body. Your body tells me things that your mind doesn't. And from there, I will literally move energy around you and away from you."

She nodded. I pointed out how she was holding her breath and asked her to breathe. I automatically knew she hadn't stopped holding her breath since the day that caused her all of the pain she was carrying. If she was an animal, it was like she was trapped and alone with her leg caught in a furrier's trap. Her heart beat wildly in fear, waiting for yet another horrible occurrence.

"This works best if we work together in a dialogue," I explained. The conversation helps me gauge what a client is willing or ready to hear, accept, acknowledge, and speak, to help with healing. Sometimes a client comes to my office to be heard. Being seen and heard are the first two steps in their healing process. I could feel Shane was ready to let go of her pain, but she was also afraid, because this pain defined her. She wasn't sure who she was without it.

She began to speak, and my heart began to break, and my breathing became difficult; I felt her shame and anger. My body took on the sensations in her physical, emotional, and spiritual body. My skin felt taut as if it was the only thing holding me together, and it was weak and thin from years of controlling shame. She wanted to hide from her past, but it was her past that she had to let go of by facing it. Holding on to the painful, defining moment was eating her from the inside out.

When I told her I saw her pain and grief, it gave her permission to open the release valve. Tears flooded from her eyes, her straight shoulders sagged, and she wept. She was still beautiful, but no longer made of stone, and she was full of self-loathing and guilt.

She loved a man who was in the process of getting divorced. This man cheated on his ex-wife and my client and now had a child with a third woman. He filled my client's head with stories of his vulnerability and declared his love while actively cheating on her.

She was afraid to leave him. Her anger about being cheated on was projected onto the woman who had his

11

baby and not the man who had done her wrong. She was not the kind of woman men cheated on.

I felt her cool façade was a skill long practiced, and, in my gut, I felt her desperate longing to feel loved as a child and her willingness to accept whatever "love" was doled out by her parents. She knew what being emotionally and spiritually neglected felt like, and she wasn't going to let her true feelings of unworthiness come to the surface — hence her controlled appearance.

"If I told you a story about a girl whose boyfriend cheated and blamed the other woman, what would you say?" I asked her.

"It takes two to tango," she responded.

"I want to help you free yourself from the hatred filling your body. All of that anger will lead to illness," I said. I understood she wasn't ready to let go of her unhealthy relationship. The empathy she deserved to give herself, the time to grieve the loss of the man she thought she loved, and the ability to see the man for who he actually was, not who she wished he would be – all of this was going to be a process. Healing a pattern or a situation doesn't happen in a single, hour-long session. It takes time and work inside my office and out of it.

During sessions, I feel the truth. This truth is received from a loving source. The truth feels like knowing the answers without ever studying. It is like knowing your friend's favorite flower and having one to give her at the exact moment she needs it. The truth always makes me cry.

For the rest of the session, I unraveled the energetic binds that held her in place. We healed her disappointment. I taught her how to forgive herself. We cut the cords that connected her to him.

I reached my heart out to her and filled the room with peacefulness to make way for the waves of shame and guilt that came spilling out of her. She sobbed so hard, her body shook, and she said, "I can't stop hating her."

I sent energy to her that I call "love and light." I told her hating the woman was only adding poison to her life. The hate was stealing energy away from her work and her future.

"There's no going back in time. He's the one who was talking to that person behind your back. He decided to go over to her house. They had sex. She got pregnant. He did that while you were his emotional support during his divorce. He doesn't sound like a great guy. You deserve better," I said.

"You're right," she said. "It's not fair."

I held my hands above her heart and called upon Mary Magdalene and angels to free her from her wounds. I felt how Shane didn't live because she was stuck in blame. It defined her and kept her imprisoned.

"It's not your fault," I told her. I asked her to imagine a cord connecting her to the other woman. I asked her to see if it was made of steel or rope. Then I asked her to see it being destroyed. I asked for healing to come to the places in her body where the cord was attached. To fill the emptiness with love and forgiveness. She was receptive to the energy work. Her body relaxed. She started to breathe. Tears ran from her eyes as her body purged the darkness.

I asked for help and guidance from the highest of loving powers, and I then became a vessel through which the healing messages and energy could travel. Her pain looked like murky shadows spilling out of her.

13

Her heart chakra wasn't spinning as it should. I then added a spark of love in the center to warm it, much like adding a flame to the center of a large block of ice.

I gave her tools to manage the pain – actionable exercises to free and forgive herself. I removed negative energy and added energetic flashes back into her chakra centers. It's similar to removing a dam in a river, allowing the water to flow naturally.

A little while later, she sat up, and her eyes had a new sparkle. Her nose was red, and her hair was less perfect.

"Thank you," she said. "I feel like I've had the best rest. I feel lighter." She smiled, and she looked bewildered and satisfied. I could see her energetically scanning her own body and auric field for what she'd released.

"Don't go looking for what you let go of. Fill yourself up with love and joy instead. Don't call the darkness back. You don't want it anymore, right?"

"Right."

I hugged her. Everything about her energetic body was lighter. She no longer dragged the chains of her past with her everywhere she went. With the gifts I have been given, I was able to heal her so she could move forward and find a loving relationship.

Can you help me heal resentment toward my family?

Yes, I can help heal the past and enable you to create healthy boundaries around people, so when they act out, it doesn't trigger you like it always has.

Soraya found me by searching the internet. She had been in therapy for years, but she knew she needed something different.

The moment she stepped into my office, she smiled. "It feels different in here than the rest of the building."

"I know. I work hard at that," I replied.

I do work hard to set and create loving and supportive energy in my office. It's furnished with two club chairs and a sunlit window. I have salt lamps placed around the room and two large tapestries hanging on my walls. One is of a large elephant in hues of orange and blue; the other depicts seven chakras.

Chakras are the energetic centers of the body. This image of a person and their chakras is set upon a background of cosmic energy. White lines swoop and swirl into geometric shapes and little stars. I point this image out to each client the first time they see me, and I explain how I see the energy around them. It moves with life and color. When those colors are gray or dark, and when there is no movement, I know those are the energies that need to be worked on in the physical body during a session.

Soraya was bold and strong from the time we met. Her perfectly lined bold bright-pink lipstick made a statement. There was no missing her when she walked into the room. Besides her boldness, there was something else evident when I met her: she seethed with anger. She enjoyed slapping her unhappiness onto the people around her in the form of judgment and derision. My body felt all of this. My shoulders tensed, I got a headache, I felt myself clench my jaw, and my mind began to spin. I sensed how she planned to dominate a conversation even before she spoke.

However, strong people don't intimidate me, and she was open to receive healing, despite her posturing. When Soraya sat down, she and I enjoyed an instant rapport. I felt she carried a secret, and I knew she wanted to change, but her unwillingness to let go of the things that have happened to her were making it impossible for her. When I looked at her, her energy was like a hoarder hiding inside her packed house. Soraya held on to *every instance* someone did something she didn't like, and every single time a person judged her. She became what she hated: an intolerant know-it-all.

I listened to her and made sure to maintain eye contact and let her see the compassion I felt for her, along with the compassion the world she wasn't able to see had for her. The healing energy I feel never judges a person for their human frailty. I believe we come into the world to learn lessons, and the divine wants to help us learn them and move on.

This is what I call "holding space." It's an energy that fills my office and is visible to those who can't see all the things I see, but they can feel it coming from my eyes and body. I held this safe space for Soraya — I wanted her to say everything she needed to let out but didn't trust anyone else to hear. She unloaded her story in the room, and I asked the loving universal energy to take it away from her.

But she didn't let go of it. How could she let go of the very thing she used to define and justify how she moved through the world? Energetically, to me, it felt like I was holding my breath while balling up my fists and trying not to lose control of tears I had held back for decades.

Why didn't she let go of her story? Because the story defined her. Who was she without the construct of being the daughter who wasn't wanted? Who was she if she wasn't the ugly sister or the one her mother emotionally abused? What kind of person would she be without resentment turning her blood red?

I took small steps forward with her to see what she was willing and able to do. She told me therapy didn't work for her. That she found my website and knew I could help her. I asked her about feeling invisible in her family. I asked if she'd ever felt seen.

"I don't want to talk about that. I don't want to talk about the past," she said. Her voice took on the tone of a child being scolded. "I only want to talk about work," she said.

She wanted to control the healing process. She mistakenly believed that if she decided what we talked about, she could continue to avoid all of those things piled up around her, burying her shine and happiness.

"How's that working for you?" I asked. My voice was soft, and I smiled.

"It's not," she admitted. All terseness left her tone, and she smiled back. "You're good," she said. "I get it."

I gave her one of my favorite life coach and author, Iyanla Vanzant, quotes, "You can't heal it if you can't name it."

In the next session, Soraya came in with a question: "Why isn't it all better?"

"It's a process. I make you sign paperwork saying you understand I can't cross my arms in front of myself and blink like a genie — and before you know it, 'poof! You're all better.' You have to do the work *outside* of the room, too. It's not just up to me."

She didn't like that. She was ready to give her power away so that healing could be easy. But growing pains have the word "pain" right in them. I know they suck. Trust me. I get it. No one likes feeling sad, and forgiveness isn't the easiest thing to do. But I believe when we feel the feeling instead of running away from the it, we end up being happier on the other side. When we avoid feeling something, by running from it, or hiding in schoolwork, helping others, shopping, binging on Netflix, drinking, or trying to be perfect, we make the loss, trauma, and pain worse. It plants itself in our bodies and minds, and it festers.

We spent the next session talking about her family's pathology. Her mother denied Soraya clothes and often ignored her and told her she was ugly. Her mother switched between being hot and cold toward her. Her mother took nice clothes away, then told Soraya she looked terrible. We touched on her sister who lived at home with their mother, and how codependent that relationship was, and how jealous she was that they were close and she was on the outside.

The energy around Soraya was dark gray. It didn't move. She made sure to be noticed out in the world in her bright colors, not out of a sense of self-empowerment and self-embodiment, but out of a desperate desire to be seen. She was a little girl playing dress-up in her mother's clothes, the same clothes her mother took from her. Soraya earned enough money to afford brand names and labels, and she made sure to be seen in them, but she gained weight from all of the stress she carried. Colorful displays of clothing would no longer control the emotional weight; the weight of her pain was literally growing on her body.

The good news was that she trusted me. I talked to her with no judgment, only compassion. She felt the universal energy of love in the room, and she wanted to hold that more than the pain to which she was clinging.

She was conditioned by her life experiences to attach herself to the pain, and I demonstrated how that wasn't her only choice. She wanted to incorporate softness and love she was accepting while working with me and find a way to make it a part of the rest of her life.

She dug in and did the Holly's Healing Homework I assigned her. She was able to receive joy and moved away from searching for what she was used to, to what she wanted. Together we created new habits, and with practice, she moved on. She got a new job. She created healthy boundaries with her family. She also found a relationship that lifted her spirit as much as she did her partner's.

What's the first step?

You need to shift how you perceive yourself and the world you live in.

I like to say: it isn't whether the glass is half-empty or full, but how many glasses you're holding and how long you've been holding on to them.

I know what it's like to have a person inside wanting to come out, and all the while have no idea how to get past the fear to do it. I understand secrets. I know what it's like to believe your parents' emotions are more important than your own. I stuffed my feelings down, first with food and then with alcohol. I know the trick of excelling in school and work and being a mess of a person at home. I know what it's like to look in the mirror and hate what you see.

I decided to write this book because I want you to heal emotional wounds to make better choices and stop perpetuating a system of beliefs about yourself that are wrong, steeped in emotional and spiritual pathology, pain, and fear. Instead of repeating patterns, I want you to make new ones, and I want you to love yourself through the process.

I talk a lot about myself and the things I experienced in my lifetime. I share them to demonstrate that I'm not a person you'd find on a mountaintop meditating and gaining holy insight. Despite my intuitive gifts, I'm a woman who went through some hard times and didn't let the horrible things define me. Yes, they impacted me in a way that altered my world view and behavior, and I worked hard to learn my lessons and heal my wounds. I sit here as an example that you, too, can survive and thrive in life. You can grow past what you know and into your own gifts. Wash that face, get rid of the masks that no longer serve you, moisturize, and get ready to love yourself.

If you have these gifts, why did you go through hard times in your life?

When I was young, I always lamented *Why me?* I said it so often my mother found Garfield's poster asking that question, and we hung it in my room.

The answer is, why not me? One of my core beliefs is that we come into this life agreeing to learn specific lessons. I think my soul has a twisted sense of humor, and while God gave me a list of things for my soul to experience and work on, I said, "Yeah! Add that, and some of that. Yes, I agree to help those souls with their trauma, and they can help me learn the lesson of forgiveness. Why not throw a few hard relationships in, and some loss, and we'll call it a day."

God said, "You sure?"

My soul laughed, and I said, "Yes!"

And here I am. We come into this world to experience everything this planet has to offer. We come in to make it better, and we have individual strengths and struggles and the ability to come out on the other side with new perspectives armed with spiritual, emotional, mental, and physical growth. We are not here to be stagnant.

What if I don't know how to define what's wrong?

This book will help you even when the pain is undefinable. I want to help you heal and construct a healthy sense of self and free you of scar tissue that alters who you are.

What's the most common issue you help heal?

All of my adult clients have some unaddressed childhood pain.

This pain is a wound or belief you keep buried, that you are afraid to tell anyone about, out of fear that you will be judged. You fret about what you are responsible for in life. This pain is a scream you muffled with both hands over your mouth for years, sometimes decades. You have a wound you are numbing with over-eating, drinking, or possibly your sexuality. The pain is a secret you must cover up with make-up, tattoos, piercings, or maybe lies. Your childhood experiences led you down the road of unhealthy relationships with partners and friends.

You lose all sense of self because you grew up learning how to please and twist yourself into Celtic knots to survive. Is every pain insurmountable? Is every pain a negative life-altering experience? To you, it is. It has stopped you from believing in yourself and taught you how to create a persona to hide it.

Today you have the option of cultivating many personas: one at home, one in school, one (or many) online, while the lucky ones have developed a sense of self and are real. Most of the time, it can be confusing to know what being real is, let alone what it feels like to love the magnificent person you are.

Do I have to heal every wound at once?

No, you don't. We can work on what you're ready to work on. Healing is a process, and you must take it one step at a time. When you fix one thing that doesn't work, you'll gain confidence in healing the next. There is no timetable for healing. Go at your own pace.

This book will take a step-by-step approach, very similar to the office visits I described earlier, where I'll help you define who you are versus the person you may pretend to be. I will create a safe place on the page to explore your feelings and unravel yourself from the issues that are tying up your sense of self. Together, you and I will uncover who you are and how you define yourself. I will open your eyes to family pathology and how you are recreating that dynamic in your friendships.

Real, Not Perfect: How to Become Your Happy, Authentic Self is a guide to loving yourself through change. I selected topics that are universal to my clients. It's a journey to accept who you are and want to be. It will address how to protect and nurture your true self. This includes instructions about setting boundaries, learning to say, "No," and other self-care tools. I will address the images and information you are exposed to twenty-four hours a day/seven days a week and demonstrate how it's all marketing bullshit created to make you feel less-than, when the truth is, there is no other person on the planet like you, and that's an amazing thing.

Knowing oneself and loving oneself is a gift. The sooner you own, acknowledge, and embody who you are, the sooner you will lead a more successful and happy life.

Two

How do you define yourself?

Now that you understand who I am and how I work, let's focus on you. Remember how I began by giving examples of how I define myself? Now it's your turn. To get unstuck and move through what's making you unhappy, we have to start at the beginning. That beginning starts with the words you choose to define and label yourself. I will help you root out the negative self-talk and understand the disconnect among the issues of how you see yourself, how the world defines you, and who you really are.

Who are you?

When I look at you, I see more than your facial expression and body language. I see the combination of divine love, your soul's unique color, and the body you occupy. It's an astounding sight that is far more illuminating than what your mirror is showing you. I guide you along my intuitive healing process to help you discover the real, magnificent you.

Being a person is about becoming and growing, and being confused and doubtful about who you are is also a part of the process. I can help you learn to value and love yourself while you figure things out. Instead of being weighed down by the unknown, let's focus on what's happening now, and nurture that person. We'll begin by uncovering what doesn't work emotionally for you and lay a foundation of who you want to be, all while supporting that goal.

When was the last time you were asked, "Who are you?" Typically, people are asked, "What's your name?" or "What do you do?" and then the person asking them the question makes a determination, a judgment, or has a reaction to what they see and perceive about the answer. When I see you, I feel your energy. I know if you're hiding something, if you're sad, annoyed, happy, or bored. If you give permission, I can sense the places in your body where you hold pain and emotions that you may not even be able to name. I see colors around you and energy pulsing off of you like heat bouncing off of a summer road.

I see the person in front of me, not the daughter or partner of someone, or the star employee, the struggling student, or the misfit, and not the mask you wear, but you as you show up. I'm a fresh set of eyes to help you tap back into who you are and feel safe being yourself.

So how do you define yourself?

HOLLY'S HEALING TIP
Never define yourself in words that diminish or belittle.

Does asking you to say who you are cause you anxiety, or do you feel an opportunity to be real? I want you to be real. Being authentic and honest about yourself is a big deal.

The world is geared toward image now more than ever. Instagram, Tik Tok, and all those apps on your phone were created to alter how you look, and perhaps project an alternate you into the world.

The questions I want you to ask yourself are:

Are you trying to be who others want you to be?

Are you trying to live up to other people's expectations?

You may not know how to answer these questions, or maybe answering them makes you feel heavy with anxiety, grief, anger, resentment, fear, or pride.

That is what this journey is about: discovering who you are minus all of the pressures you navigate daily. Remember, who you are should NOT fundamentally change depending on who you are with at any given time. Some of your behaviors may change, like what you say or won't say in front of friends versus an employer, but who you are at the core of you is the same.

Let me break this down further. There is a huge difference between character and personality.

Character is defined as the mental and moral qualities of a person.

Personality is defined as an embodiment of a collection of qualities.

Your character is who you are at your core, whereas the personality you often meet can be a mask worn by an individual. It is meant to deflect or hide behind, to draw you in, or to please others.

Have you known a person who appears to be attractive or dazzling in some way, only to find out later on that they are mean, cruel, and not what they seem? That's precisely what I'm mentioning. The dazzling part is personality, and the mean and nasty part is the person's real character shining through.

You may wear a personality mask or two in your life. Your professional, parent, or student persona, or how you act as a sister, athlete, artist, or nerd may help you get through your day, but we want to get to the very core of you — the hidden part that holds your insecurities and stress. I want to help bolster that part of you so you can love and protect it.

Write the answers to my questions in a separate notebook or journal or use the space provided throughout the book. Writing things by hand is part of the process. You're meant to slow down and think about your answers. Long hand answers will connect you to your emotions in a visceral way. I want you to be in your body and stay aware of your thoughts. It's time to sort them out. Ready? Here we go...

HOLLY'S HEALING HOMEWORK:

In the space provided, or in a separate notebook, complete the following:

Write all of the words you use to define yourself.

Write all of the words you think other people use to define you.

Write all of the words you heard your family uses to define you.

Write all of the words advertising uses to define you.

Write all of the words social media uses to define you.

Rewrite all of the words that appear in more than one list.

How many of those words are hurtful or damaging to you? Which ones?

How many of the words you wrote down do you consider to be true in defining you? Rewrite those words here.

Would you ever post a picture that wasn't flattering or somehow altered?

On a scale of 1-10, one being the lowest, how much do you like yourself and your character? Why?

Look at all of the words you wrote down that embody negative self-talk. How much do you believe them? I wonder if you were conditioned to think this about yourself. It's time to say, "Goodbye!" to them.

Write all of the negative self-talk words on a white sheet of paper. Then, tear them up. Completely destroy them.

Take all of the positive words about yourself and write them down again. Post a few in places you'll sure to see in order to remind yourself how amazing you are. Place them on your computer screen, your bathroom mirror, and the television remote.

If you don't have any words about yourself you like, it's okay. I haven't met you, but I'm sure at least some of these will apply: You're thoughtful. You care. Animals love you. You have gorgeous eyes. You have pretty hair. I like your freckles.

HOLLY'S HEALING CHALLENGE:

Look in the mirror and find something about your physical appearance you like. It can be how curly your hair is, your strong, thick legs, the scar only you can see, the color of your eyes, your skin tone, or maybe the freckle on your nose. There is no right or wrong regarding what you like about your body and appearance.

After selecting what you like, I want you to look at yourself in the mirror and smile while looking at that aspect of you. I want you to take ownership of this physical trait and feel good about it.

Repeat this exercise three times per week.

You may discover you start to like more of your physical traits. Express yourself, and own your ability to like yourself!

Three

Who do you want to be?

When you look in the mirror, do you like what you see? Or do you spend the majority of the time wishing things were different? That *you* were different?

Well, the good news is that you are changing every day. Your body, mind, and physiology are evolving, and your soul is along for the ride.

So, what does that mean? It means that you are in the process of becoming the individual your soul is meant to become. The person inside you— the curious, energetic being who may be constrained by your surroundings— is metamorphizing into someone magnificent. Just as your body matures from infant to child, then adolescent, and adult, your mind and soul can shift and reach new energetic and spiritual levels.

Think of spiritual growth as exercise for your soul. The benefits of exercise to your physical and mental well-being are widely known. Muscles become tone, while aches and pains diminish, and your confidence increases. You're probably happy and feeling good about life.

Together we can do similar work for your spiritual well-being. It all starts with your willingness to change what no longer serves you, and to start loving yourself.

HOLLY'S HEALING TIP
It's okay to not know everything about yourself.
It's okay to take your time and figure things out.

You matter. Who you are is important. You don't have to be anything other than you. It seems logical and straightforward when you read those words, doesn't it? But the truth is, it can be challenging, confusing, overwhelming, and awkward growing into yourself.

I've always had a sense of who I was and am, but that doesn't mean it was stress-free or an easy road for me to travel. However, every time I tried to please another person, tried to conform in ways that made me less-than to fit in, I felt like I was lying. I wasn't happy being part of the group or even being around those people, because I stopped listening to my intuition and instincts and pretended to be something I wasn't. I never made it while pretending to be anything other than my quirky, dance-loving, empathetic, intuitive, creative self for more than a week. That means that even though I didn't know what was wrong or why I felt like I didn't fit in, making myself into someone I was not caused me anxiety, as well as emotional and mental fatigue.

I was never part of a clique as a child or an adult. I watched these groups of people move as one, and I observed from the outside, thinking, *What happens if someone inside the group doesn't agree with the leader? What if I don't want to go along and do everything the group does? What if I don't want to spend my time tearing others down with gossip?*

So, I didn't become part of any group. Instead, I had friends who were part of many different cliques, and some days I was lonely. Other days I was grateful. Most of the time, I enjoyed my different friends without the limitations created by other people, who, in reality, were trying to figure things out themselves. I didn't need a group to define me. I chose to express myself even when I wasn't one hundred percent sure of who I was.

For those of you trying to sort out your feelings about yourself, may to ask, when you were little, who did you imagine you'd be when you grew up?

There are a million ways to define who you are at any given moment. But instead of searching for a brand from the outside to define yourself, I want you to turn inward.

HOLLY'S HEALING TIP
Your truth comes from within.
Your soul can't be defined by fads, fashions, or trends.

I think that some labels hurt a person, making you choose what you are while you're still growing. People are not rocks. We don't come into existence to remain one thing. For instance, the world is full of gender and sexuality options.

Look at adolescence. You metamorphize from child to adult. Hormones change you, both mentally and physically. Why not think of yourself as becoming? Take the pressure off of having to be something specific, and just be you. It's harder than you think. I'm not going to sugarcoat it. Being an individual can be a scary thing. People tend to judge others when they feel uncomfortable or don't understand. But so what? Nothing feels better than being authentic. It's a gift you can give the world, and helping you get there my greatest desire.

The thing people say to me after they meet me tends to be, "You're so authentic."

I always blush and take it in. Being authentically me has its challenges and rewards. Let me tell you a bit about my journey to this point. Once upon a time, I was a people pleaser. The role I claimed within my nuclear family dynamic was the bridge. I believed it was my job to smooth things over between people and be exceptionally good, so no one had a reason to be upset.

I didn't have coping skills. My mother taught me how to present an image of beauty in the world. And when she is angry, she is passive-aggressive, goes silent, and seethes. My father was a raging alcoholic for much of my life. When I say raging, what I mean is his body would thrum and shake with hostility and rage. He would scream and yell over little things, and I can recall with perfect clarity how spit hurled from his mouth while he roared.

In response to my environment, I became as self-sufficient as humanly possible. I never asked for help. I was an over-achiever in school and whatever sport I played. I picked friends who were smart, but damaged. I believe the pain inside me reached out to connect to the hurt inside of them.

And I was still fiercely individualistic. I got older and married a broken man. I believed if I loved him enough, I could make him happy. I was a victim of my own story. I perpetuated the beliefs of making myself "less-than" so I could make someone else feel better. During my twenties, I didn't own my creativity. I gave my ideas away to others; they took credit, and I got angry. I worked hard, and at twenty-eight, I burned out.

HOLLY'S HEALING TIP
Don't become what you hate.
Be who you are meant to be.

I realized that what I thought I knew as my truth wasn't working for me. I was what I learned, but I wasn't who I was meant to be. I started the process of healing old wounds, picking up all of the pieces of myself that had gotten pecked off and devoured by others' needs. I had to learn how to ask for help. I took care of myself and made choices based on my healing self. I began learning how to set boundaries. I found my voice, and I've made sure to exercise it ever since.

How can you figure yourself out? There are plenty of ways. First off, there's nothing wrong with dreaming.

HOLLY'S HEALING HOMEWORK:

Close your eyes and notice how you're sitting. Pay attention to the way your body presses against the chair and how your legs are arranged. Notice your breath but don't change how you are breathing. Take a deep breath in and let it out. Make the sound, *aahhhh*. Do it two more times. Breathe in and out.

Next, with your eyes still closed, imagine looking at a reflection of yourself; it will be the best version of you. It is your soul looking back at you. Open your eyes and take the time to write down what you saw and experienced.

What did you look like?

Did you appear how others see you or could you see your highest self?

Were you doing something?

Did your reflection smile back at you?

Did you like seeing your soul reflected back at you?

Could you feel the unconditional love in your eyes?

Was the love overwhelming?

Did you believe it possible to feel so confident about yourself?

The version of you looking back is your soul and divine energy.

God may be a tricky subject. There are so many ways to pray to God as well as religious ceremonies designed to organize prayer. For this book's purposes, I'm going to define God as unconditional, loving energy to which your soul is connected.

GUIDED MEDITATION

Do you meditate? I think people say they do when they don't because meditation can be intimidating. But the whole point of meditation is the antithesis of intimidation. Meditation is all about being in the moment. It's called a mindful practice not because your mind runs wild with things that need to be done, worries, or the last song you heard, but because it's about giving your mind a little time off and giving yourself permission to quiet all of those wild thoughts ricocheting around inside your head.

Let me introduce meditation to you. There are many ways in which a person can meditate. Don't allow anyone to tell you that what works for you is wrong, and don't believe the only way to meditate is with your legs in lotus pose and your palms facing up. I don't believe there's one right way to meditate. I define meditation as a mindful practice, when a person is singularly focused and not allowing the noise of the outside world to interfere.

People can meditate while walking in the woods, playing golf, at the range, at the beach, in the bath, at yoga — the possibilities are endless. The most important thing to remember is to unplug from your phone and all electronic devices while meditating.

For this first attempt at meditation, I want you to read the entire written meditation before trying it. Do not judge yourself on a skill you are only beginning to practice. Meditate where you have privacy and quiet. Get in a comfortable resting position, either seated or lying down. Notice any feelings that come up at the start. Do you feel silly, anxious, or are you eager to relax? Do you notice any tension in your body? Is your to-do list growing as you sit and think?

These are normal reactions. You may acknowledge them without guilt. Shift your attention back to your breath. Notice how you inhale and exhale without changing it. Settle into the moment, the location, the here and now.

I want you to imagine yourself at your favorite place. The place can be real or imagined. You may not have ever been there before — it doesn't matter. Maybe you're at a beach with your feet in the sand, or floating on top of the water, or you are under your covers, in a childhood fort, or high up on a mountain trail. You may even be in the middle of a forest listening to the sounds of the wind rustling the leaves, or floating in the sky on top of clouds while sunshine warms your face. Stay in your chosen place. Feel the peace of it sink into your body. Allow the muscles in your neck and shoulders to ease and relax. Notice if your favorite place has specific smells or sounds. Let your five senses connect you to your chosen space in time. Know you are safe, and nothing can hurt you. Take a deep breath in, open your mouth, and let it out.

Next, breathe in peace. Then, exhale judgment. Breathe in acceptance and breathe out "I should be's." Breathe in light and exhale darkness. You are in a safe place, willing to heal.

I want you to imagine drawing soothing energy up from the earth and in through the soles of your feet. The energy will move past your feet, up your legs, into your shins, past your thighs, and into your torso. It may tingle or feel solid in your body.

Next, the healing energy will travel up, past your belly button, into your heart, into your throat and the back of your head, past your mouth and eyes, and to the very top of your head. This energy is you being grounded in your safest place, your personal sanctuary. Please make sure your hands are face down and also drawing the energy of your place into your body.

This grounding and healing will happen without any effort on your part. If you don't feel it, that's fine. Your will does not control healing. Your acceptance does. Get comfortable in the not doing. There is no need to rush. Enjoy the support in and around you. The grounded soothing energy that fills this favorite space is God. God's love for you is unconditional. It's always there to help and heal.

When you're ready, I want you to invite your highest self to join you. To do this, all you have to think is *I want to connect with my highest self. I am open to receive this loving connection.* Imagine your highest self walks over and sits in front of you. You are face-to-face. Be open to see what you are at your soul level. God and your highest self love you completely and utterly, without limits. Take in what it feels like to be loved this way. Imagine the center of your heart receiving the greatest love and joy, the warmest, most honest hug, and the kindness for which you long.

Stay and enjoy the sensations. You may notice tears well up. You may be overwhelmed by the sense of acceptance. You may see how beautiful you are. Or this may be a challenging exercise. No matter what, all of it is okay. Remember, meditation is a skill that requires practice.

Take three more slow breaths in and out. Look at your reflection and thank it. Thank God for being able to connect you to this experience. Then, when you are ready to reconnect to the world, place your left hand over your heart and your right hand over your left. End the meditation with gratitude. Be grateful for the time you gave yourself. Be grateful for connecting to the source/God and your highest self. I always say, "Amen," at the end of meditations. If that feels natural to you, I encourage you to do the same.

Know that the love and grounding energy stays with you after you end the meditation, and this meditation is always available for you to return to it. Smile, because you did it. You successfully grounded and got quiet.

Open your eyes and answer these questions:

What did the soul level version of you look like?

How did it feel to be seen?

Did your reflection smile back at you?

Did you like seeing your soul reflected back at you?

Did you feel the unconditional love in those eyes?

Was the love overwhelming?

Did you believe it possible to feel so confident about yourself?

Was it the most authentic self you long to be?

Did the place and the version of you which you saw cause anxiety, or peace?

What did the version of you which you saw want to know?

How was the version's voice different than the one you speak with regularly?

What did you need to hear the most?

HOLLY'S HEALING TIP
Your soul is patient. Don't rush the healing process.

This version of you is always available. It's the part of you I see. If you need to do this exercise several times to become comfortable being seen and loved, that's okay. There is no right way to heal, and your highest self isn't going anywhere. The soul is patient and ready to support you whenever you want to connect with it.

Four

What are you afraid of?

The journey to be the best version of you starts with an honest look at yourself. However, please don't confuse honesty with unkind scrutiny. Remember, you are here to heal, not inflict harsh judgments. I want you to begin to decipher the internal and external forces that work together to create your perception of yourself.

My experience is that fear is the most significant inhibitor of change. Fear is tricky, and it can camouflage itself and be manipulative. Let me demonstrate how well fear can hide, and then inhabit your mind, body, and soul. Fear is such an asshole.

I thought about writing this book for over a year before starting the journey to put one word after the other on paper. My literary agent asked me to write it for a teen audience, so I said, "Yes, of course. I can do that." Then I had to learn how to write a book proposal and the rest of the process for writing a non-fiction book.

Someone suggested I read other self-help books and gave me some bestselling authors as suggestions for reading material. I read a few but couldn't relate to their advice because it felt like I was reading marketing material. My eyes glazed over. I put my business cards in the self-help books in local bookstores because I thought I could be more helpful than those particular books. I created an outline for this book and decided what I planned to include.

HOLLY'S HEALING TIP
Not every opportunity is a good one.

During the same time, I was invited to speak in front of a large audience. I was selected because of my personality and what I had to say about boundaries. During the months that led up to the speaking engagement, the person in charge kept giving me notes on how not to be "so Holly," including not using my hands so much, not being self-deprecating, not moving my feet a certain way, not using the PowerPoint slides I had selected, not doing this or that. Above all, I was being told to stop being *me*.

I tried to please the person organizing the event by making myself smaller and less me. I became more and more nervous; every time I opened my mouth or did something, I heard her voice. I got notes on a talk that the person had never actually listened to, and the critique never included a kind word of encouragement.

Guess what happened? The two situations created an internal explosion. Old doubts and fears made me sick. I ended up in urgent care, getting X-rays for walking pneumonia.

Here is what the fear said to me: *This is an opportunity, and I better not fuck it up. I have to work harder than ever before to make sure my agent and a publisher love this book. I have to work hard for the person who asked me to speak at her event, so she loves what I have to say. I better take every note she gives me and tailor my demeanor to be "professional enough" for her.*

In short, I stopped being me, which is crazy, because I'm really good at being me.

Not every opportunity is a good one. And I was writing and creating content with a filter of fear.

The fear was:

My perspective wasn't as valid as those of others.

They have to like the content.

Their opinions are more important than mine.

They know better than me.

Instead, I should have said, "No. You asked for me, and this is me."

I began writing this book while I was afraid to say what I feel. I tried using all of my intuitive gifts and magical "Clair" abilities to know what my readers wanted. I was worried I might upset a teenager's parents if they saw this book and disapproved of what I wrote. I was afraid my readers' issues wouldn't be addressed. I was scared of saying it the wrong way, and having my words fail me. Fear disguised itself as impostor syndrome.

It took a dream I had for me to finally get the message. In the dream, I felt something in my hair. I combed my fingers through my hair, and all of these tiny snakes fell onto a table. They were harmless baby garter snakes.

"How did they get there?" I asked while still in my dream.

"They fell from the trees," I was told.

There were about fifteen snakes on the table. One baby snake coiled up and pulled itself up and stared at me. He was an inch or two long, and he made direct eye contact with me. I leaned over to get a better look at this defiant snake, and I saw the tiniest rattle at the end of his tail. The snake shook it at me. He was annoyed with me. He didn't blink, and neither did I.

When I woke up from the dream, I understood that little snake. I understood how the disguised fears in me, from the fear of not being good enough, to the fear of not being liked or well-received, had taken over my creativity.

I understood I'd been writing the wrong book for ten months. The fear of saying something wrong stifled me, but when I remembered I am fearless in my practice, I knew I must be brave as a writer, an intuitive, and a speaker.

I don't shirk away from who I am in general. I love myself, but there it was, fear dressed up as: *this is what you need to do to be successful.*

I may choose my words carefully when working with a client, but I also stumble over words, and I have typos in almost everything I write. This is who I am, so I'm particularly grateful for editors! It doesn't mean my writing or insights aren't good; it means I'm not a grammar expert. I'm intense and soft. I am more than one thing, and figuring out who you are means shedding limiting beliefs and loving *all of you.* The good and the imperfect. It's about changing the things that no longer serve you or work for you, and love the rest.

There's no such thing as perfect, but there's the you you want to be, and fear will take your place in the mirror and say mean shit. Fear will tell you, "You don't deserve it." Fear will say "No, in myriad ways. Fear will come out of your friends' mouths when they see you move away or stop a self-destructive pattern. Fear will enunciate words and sound like advice from parents and well-meaning people. Fear is so sly.

Fuck fear.

Once I saw how I was a sucker to the fear of not doing it right, I was free to be me.

This book and my perspective may not be right for everyone, but I know that it is the book I'm meant to write and share with every fiber of my being. And that's how you beat fear. You hold onto your truth, and you shimmy past that host of reasons not to, and get on with living.

What does fear do to you? How does fear dull your shine?

HOLLY'S HEALING TIP
Do you. Be you.
It feels worse to live your life
like the person others want you to be than to be your
own self, authentic and capable of failure.
The other version erodes self-esteem and erases your
individuality.

I've always been who I am. I just wasn't fully formed, and therefore had wiggle room to figure myself out and make some mistakes. The things I knew about myself included how:

I saw the world differently than others.

I love to dance.

I believed with every fiber of my being that it was my job to make people in my family happy.

For a while, I was convinced I was an alien, or at the very least, abducted by aliens (I had a recurring nightmare about being taken into space).

I didn't know how to process my feelings and used dance to express everything.

I was afraid of disappointing anyone.

I didn't understand why being myself put a target on me.

I never liked mean people.

I always heard my inner voice, felt the tugs and pulls of my inner strength, but didn't always know what to do with them.

What do you know for sure about yourself? Write it down here:

What frightens you?

As a child, you may have been frightened of the dark. The unknown and unseen may have set off anxiety in your body. Where others felt a rush, you may have felt terror.

I was deathly afraid of the dark. Looking back, I believe it's because I saw things in the darkness, felt the presence of other beings, and had gifts I didn't know how to explain. It didn't help that I didn't have anyone to help explain what was going on inside me. I will never forget the feeling of wondering *what's hiding in the dark?*

As a student, I was always afraid of doing poorly in school. I over-achieved and did what I could to achieve an A average. My mother says she never had to pressure me about school because I did it all myself.

When I started to work, I was afraid of making mistakes, as if the error would land me inside an iron maiden, tortured, or fired. I believed mistakes defined me as less-than, and I was always about proving myself to the outside world while secretly thinking I didn't measure up in my inner world.

All of those fears stopped me from exploring myself for a time. Each fear festered inside of me, keeping me from reaching for the stars.

I see many people who are afraid of change. They're scared to feel their feelings for fear that moving through emotions will destroy the carefully constructed image and persona they've crafted. People are afraid of hurting other people or being a disappointment. We fear rejection, and many of us fear being alone, even if the relationship is toxic and unhealthy.

Fear is anxiety-producing and an all-stop for most people I meet. Clients come in unhappy and dissatisfied, and some come with rage, while others harbor enormous grief. Fear keeps them stuck, because most people would rather stay in a situation they know than one they don't. People lean on coping mechanisms instead of leaning forward and breaking through.

Fear is no joke. I'm not being flippant or dismissive. But I know from experience that nothing good comes from living a life filled with fear.

I do my best to face and conquer my fears. Zip-lining made me face my fear of heights. This fear can manipulate my mind and body. Heights involuntarily cause me severe vertigo. I become convinced I'm going to fall; then my body shakes, and I cry and sweat. Vertigo distorts my vision, makes objects swirl, and the ground moves from low to high, literally making me lose my balance. Panic sweeps through my physical body, making my armpits sweat with the stink of fear, all while my hands get sweaty, I become nauseated, and I'm sure I will fall to my death. I know I sound dramatic, but it's all so real for me.

I'm afraid of driving over bridges and have to be in the middle lane, so those same involuntary reactions don't overcome my ability to steer my car.

Snakes freak me out, and so do spiders (although I'm not afraid of spiders in the house, and I'm the one to catch them in a cup and fling them outside where they belong).

My favorite definition of fear I've seen is:

False
Evidence
Appearing
Real

Fear is tricky. It can disguise its voice inside your head.

HOLLY'S HEALING TIP
Don't let fear rule your life.

Fear of failure stops people from trying new things. But guess what? You fell a lot when you learned to walk. You didn't know how to ride a bicycle and crush doing pop-a-wheelies. You had to learn the ABCs before you could read. Learning a new skill requires mastering small steps before you advance to the next ones. When you get the knack for one thing, your confidence goes up, and the next step isn't as scary. If you let the fear stop you, then you're living a half-life.

You reached for this book because part of you is ready and willing to change. Now it's time to name your fears and face them. I know you are brave enough to meet and heal them.

FOR READERS STILL IN SCHOOL:

The world is at your fingertips. Social media brings many more sets of eyes and opinions. You are under so much more pressure than I ever knew. What's worse is how people can be bullies while being anonymous in apps and on the internet. I wish I had the antidote for meanness that you could put in the water to make people kinder. Heck, I wish I could sprinkle that magic potion worldwide, but that kind of magic is not anything I can conjure. What I can do is help you feel better about being you. Then, when you encounter bullies, you won't be as affected by them.

I felt good about what I knew about myself, and I preferred being called the weird one rather than making myself dumber to fit in with a clique. Outside forces didn't influence who I was so much as made me feel wrong about not being thinner or more popular. But none of that stopped me from wearing purple shoes, changing hairstyles when I wanted, and trying new make-up and fashion.

That isn't the case for everyone. Knowing who you are doesn't mean you can walk about the world being comfortable being you. There's so much judgment. There are so many other people telling you what's right and wrong. Countless outside influences can impact your self- confidence.

Peer pressure is real. All of the whispers and text messages about how you look and what you say are real. I understand it can be challenging to navigate the pressure to fit in, especially if you don't have close friends to lean on. Friendship is important. Parental support is helpful, too. Most parents are honestly doing their best to love and support their children. They can only do and act as good as they are. Parents are people, and people are flawed.

Friends are the family you choose. It's better to have a few real friends than a gaggle of fake ones. Fake friends add insecurity to your life. Real ones boost your self-confidence.

HOLLY'S HEALING TIP
Being your true self will feel better than
any version you pretend to be.

HOLLY'S HEALING HOMEWORK:

Let's dig deeper. It's essential to know your fears so they can be healed. Fight the urge to sugarcoat the truth, and don't beat yourself up for owning your human frailty. Answer these questions about yourself:

Is the public you different than the private you?

If there are differences, what are they?

Which version of yourself do you prefer being?

Do you believe there's a way to combine the different personas?

What's the difference between your personality and character?

How do you feel during the day?

Do you feel anxious?

How do you want to feel?

How does fear affect you?

How do you cope with fear?

How does fear hold you back?

What are you most afraid of?

Are you used to being scared?

Does fear make you hide?

When do you recall first being afraid of fear?

What emotions are connected to your fear?

Is there a person connected to your fear?

Do you need time to process the fear?

Have empathy for your fears. Beating yourself up over your emotional reactions is not what this exercise is about. We have to name things, and then accept and acknowledge them to have empathy and forgiveness for ourselves before changes can be made, and before we can work to make those changes stick.

The questions and answers above are a place to be honest and reveal your thoughts and feelings so we can build on them. It's okay if mixed emotions bubble up during the homework. Write them down. They're both valid and significant.

It's essential to know and own your fears, so we can help assuage and heal them. I'm asking you to trust me in this process. Know that your vulnerability to do the work is commended. I am so proud of you for doing so much already. It's essential to know your fears so we can focus on the right tools to help you deal with them.

If you'd like a gentle reminder of how worthy and loved you are, I suggest you get a lovely piece of rose quartz. I keep a small heart of rose quartz on my desk as a reminder that I am loved. In general, rose quartz is a stone known for its heart-healing properties, including, but not limited to, encouraging self-love, easing heartache, soothing emotional pain, and offering a sense of peace.

For those of you who are new to crystals as part of your healing, I'm going to suggest you do some of your own research. There are many websites, books, and people who specialize in teaching about crystals.

GUIDED MEDITATION

Take a deep breath in and let it out. Breathe in patience and exhale judgment. Breathe in kindness and exhale opinions. Breathe in calm and exhale nervousness.

Notice if you're clenching your jaw, and if so, try to relax it. If your shoulders are shrugged, I want you to lift them higher to your ears and sigh them down.

See if you can be quiet for fifteen seconds. It's a small amount of time to gift yourself — fifteen seconds of not doing. I know you can do it.

Now I want you to call out one of the fears you wrote down. Start with the one that popped into your mind first. I want you to give that fear a shape. The shape may be an object, whether geometric, or something like a duck or a dragon. It doesn't matter what the form is, only that you can imagine it.

If the shape is looming over you, I want you to shrink it. For example, if you imagined your fear to be a dragon, and that dragon had shiny black scales, was seething with anger, and had fire dripping from its nostrils, I want you to imagine shrinking it.

See the dragon and all of its power getting smaller and smaller until it fits in the palm of your hand. If you want to, you can put it in a little cage.

If your fear was a color, I want you to imagine a bright white light coming down from heaven and surrounding it until the color is gone and you are left with only warmth and light of love.

When you're ready, I suggest getting a white piece of paper, and then writing the fear you chose and how you saw it. After you do this, burn the paper. I want you to see the fear being visibly destroyed. Please do this in a safe container or location and keep water on hand to extinguish the flame, if needed. Please use the necessary precautions during this exercise to ensure safety.

When you are done, smile and know you took the first step in letting a fear go.

It's crucial to keep love and light in your thoughts while doing any energy work. We never want to do any meditation or ceremony with anything other than love and light. Remember, we are loving ourselves through change!

As I'm not a licensed therapist or doctor, I want to provide additional resources for you. Are you actively living in fear? If you are in a dangerous situation, please seek immediate help!

Helpful Resources:

National Domestic Violence Hotline: 1–800–799–7233 or TTY 1–800–787–3224

Childhelp National Child Abuse Hotline: 1-800-422-4453

Substance Abuse and Mental Health Services Administration, (SAMHSA) Treatment Referral Helpline: 1-877-622-4357

National Suicide Prevention Lifeline: 1-800-273-TALK (8255)

You can always dial 911 if you are in danger of hurting yourself or others.

Five

What about your friends?

This chapter was the hardest one for me to write. Revisiting my past and friendships was surprisingly emotional for me. I'd like to blame the pandemic for adding to the challenges of excavating my personal relationships, but the truth is, friendships are one lesson I'm still learning, too.

To facilitate healing, we will evaluate friendships as they appear and operate in your life. Please take your time in this chapter. There is a huge difference between people you have known for a long time and those you can call friends. Longevity doesn't equate to quality.

Your friends are a reflection of who you are and your self-worth. As you continue your journey to loving the real you, it's crucial to assess the friends you keep close, as well as those who need to be let go, all while creating space for new ones.

This process of evaluation is not done with malice or delivered with cruelty. All healing comes from a space of kindness for yourself.

Were you taught how to make friends?

I wasn't taught how to make friends. My parents didn't sit me down and say, "Holly, friends are an important part of life. They will bring you much joy and companionship. It's important to know what a friend is and what they're not."

We were taught how to make your bed, tie your shoes, and cut your food, but why weren't we taught how to make friends?

Your friends are culled from those seated near you or in the same room as you from a very early age. You made friends based around where your family lived. Your street and neighborhood were where you first met groups of children. It doesn't get more random than that. Most of your friends, prior to having mobile devices and social media, were made as a result of proximity. There was no evaluating these people. It was necessary to play with the neighbor or be lonely.

I wish my mom had sat me down and taught me the qualities friends ought to possess so I could have learned to establish healthy boundaries. This is a subject that's always appropriate and one worth revisiting with children as they grow and mature.

Here are the ground rules for friends, no matter your age:

Friends never make you feel bad about yourself.

Friends don't force you to do unsafe things.

Friends don't belittle.

Friends tell you the truth, even when the truth is hard to

hear.

Friends care about your well-being.

Friends cheer you on.

Friends check in.

Friends are fun.

This list applies to every age. It contains the basics. You can add to this list as you mature. Friends should add color to your life.

Please take a moment and assess if you truly had anything in common with your childhood friends other than geography.

Did you have to manage to find your place within that group of personalities?

What did you learn about getting along with others in your earliest friendships?

What, if any, criteria did you use to determine if your friends were actually good for your life?

In hindsight, I see how, when I was younger, I chose friends whose energy and emotional dynamics mirrored what went on behind closed doors in my house. I selected people who were wounded, needed help, and didn't necessarily have my back. I believe the wounds inside me recognized the wounds inside of them.

You may be wondering, where is there a problem with that? Your friend(s) need you, and you need them; doesn't that mean it's a symbiotic relationship?

No, no, it does not. As a matter of fact, it could lead you down a dangerous path — especially if you are a people pleaser.

Let's travel back in time in my life to better demonstrate why these pain-connected relationships can be unsafe.

In high school, I had a friend named Maria. Maria's mom was awful to her, moving my friend's bedroom into the hall closet. My friend decorated the inside of the closet with Van Halen posters, and I remember squeezing in to visit her. Maria was years ahead of me in sexual experiences, and she decided that I was too old to be a virgin at fifteen.

So, she orchestrated a plan. She invited boys over to my house when my parents were out for the day. I was a good girl, and my parents trusted me when I was home alone. Maria invited people I'd never met and who weren't in high school over to my house. Once, we were playing a game of pool and one of the guys disappeared, so I went looking for him. I found him in my parents' bedroom. He was older than I was at the time; I thought he was twenty. I never learned his name. He started kissing me, and the next thing my body remembers is staring at the blue fern wallpaper in my parents' bedroom, being pinned under him, and the sound of him putting a condom on before he had sex with me. When he was done, he got up and dressed. Thinking about this now, I have no idea what he ever did with that condom. I can distinctly recall, with vivid clarity, the bloodstain on my parents' bedspread and how my dog jumped up on the bed to lick it. I remember pulling the blanket off, but I can't recall how I cleaned it.

I was confused and stunned. What made my rapist do that? Was my cold-shoulder sweatshirt that sexy? Did I really look seventeen? When I walked out of my parents' room, I'll never forget how everyone who was still playing pool applauded.

I never told anyone what had actually happened. It took me thirteen years to share this story with my therapist, and it took her many sessions to help me understand I was raped. It took me milliseconds to comprehend how Maria had orchestrated it.

Although I wanted to lift her up and bring happiness to her life, Maria sought to level the playing field. I didn't end my friendship with her. She and I were friends until I moved away. This is one of those stories in my life that I wish I could change. I wish I could help the girl I was then, but I can't. I wish I could help the girl who was my friend, too. As an adult, I still can't fathom how hurt and broken she must have been to have done something like that to me.

And although that moment defined my sexuality until I was twenty-eight, I can tell you I did finally heal.

There may be a person in your life claiming to be your friend but who is really jealous, manipulative, and using you. That person's behavior is not your fault. Recognizing and being able to discern that the person isn't the friend you once believed they were is progress. And that's a big deal.

Fake people won't support you being real. They will probably try to sabotage what you are working for by playing on your fears.

This is where your healing comes in.

Appreciate your ability to do the healing work. And although you may be afraid to be alone, I'm here to tell you being alone is a great place to be if the other choice is being surrounded by toxic people.

When you become comfortable with yourself, you can rid yourself of all of the other versions of you that others plant in your head and heart. You can let the lies go and heal what hurts. You can take time to discover who you are and who you want to invite into your life.

Remember, friends accept you for who and what you are. They never make you feel less-than. They don't have rules to be around them, and they don't steal your boyfriends, girlfriends, money, time, ideas, or energy.

Please never beat yourself up for the "bad" choices in your life. The great thing about a decision is that you get to make another one if it doesn't work out for you. We don't arrive on the planet and experience life for it to be all easy. Life is about learning, and part of learning is making mistakes, errors, bad judgment calls, oopsies, and coming upon things that are better left forgotten. It's from those moments that we learn.

Again, it's called growing pains, not happy blooms, because it appears that humanity doesn't learn things the easy way. Pain is part of progress.

What patterns have I seen and helped heal?

Even though every person who seeks me out to heal friendships comes from many different backgrounds and life circumstances, I have seen universal patterns.

You can ask yourself this question: Are you a giver or a taker? The first pattern is a friendship in which one person is cruel and demeaning, and the other person is a people pleaser. My clients are typically the individuals trying to make other people happy with gifts, love, and kindness, while they deny how belittled they feel by doing all of the above.

There are givers and takers. The takers will take your time, energy, money, and self-worth.

The givers believe they have the ability to help the other person. I'm going to define help, in instances like these, as being able to please. Many givers feel terrible being around the taker, but they don't step away because of guilt and shame. Maybe they have known the taker for a long time. Perhaps they justify the taker's behavior by deciding the person is going through a hard time and needs love.

These are well-meaning excuses. So, let's say, for argument's sake, the taker is going through a hard time. So what? Their difficult times do not remedy the days, months, or years of unkindness they have shown you. Just because you know someone for a long time does not make them a good friend. Remember, your earliest friends were formed out of proximity, not a discerning mind.

HOLLY'S HEALING TIP
Real friends like you and accept you for who you are – warts and all.

A friend who never respects your boundaries and always makes you feel less-than is not a friend, and I say give yourself permission to remove them from your inner circle. There are degrees to which you can remove a person from your life. A person who was once in your inner circle can be moved outward when the relationship changes. You don't have to end all friendships, but you can be honest about them and how they make you feel. A simple test to evaluate things is to ask yourself, do they bring you joy, and do you feel good when you're around them?

I have a client who tells me about her old group of childhood friends. Every time she sees them, she quickly makes an appointment with me to help release her anxiety and anger. These women continue to play into their high school mean girl roles, while my client is the nice one – the one they don't respect, are mean to, and belittle with off-the-cuff remarks and backhanded compliments. I'm working with her to help her free herself from the guilt and belief that these women are her friends, when really, they aren't. They are people she grew up with and has shared memories with, but friends don't belittle friends. They are uplifting to one another.

My client had a need that kept her going back to her old friends. Her need was to be seen, accepted, and valued. She wanted them to see her as the wonderful woman she was. She wanted her creativity to be acknowledged. She wanted them to stop contacting her when they wanted things and instead call her for fun. She was perplexed as to why one woman was always rude and condescending. My client was repeating the pattern of being the insecure high school girl she once was.

The pain she struggled to let go of was the need to be seen as a good person, and her need to be appreciated. She struggled with the haunting question: Why?

Why did so-called-friends treat her so poorly? The truth was, the other people would never give her the kindness or respect she deserved because they weren't her people. They were people she knew, and it was time to let them go.

I said, "You can't get love from a rock. It's not the rock's fault. It's just a rock."

While a person is actively in a place of pain, this is a hard sentiment to accept. But once healing happens, you won't expect a rock to wrap imaginary arms around you and give you love. You'll see it for what it is. Inert.

Together we ended the pattern of wanting an emotional connection from people who can't connect and respect. I helped her see the childhood friends for who and what they were. They were not an energetic fit for her. It was time to let go and cut the cords between the girl she was and the woman she had become. So, we cut the cords of unwanted negative relationships in her life.

I help clients cut cords with people all the time. A cord is an energetic line between people. And while I do this work, I always ask that the cord reattach in a healthy way or not at all. Healthy endings don't include revenge of any kind. Releasing attachment that no longer serves you should always be done with love and light.

I don't think ending a friendship needs to be any more dramatic than letting go. I do personally block people from my private social media pages when they demonstrate they're not my friends. Why on earth would I give access to my private details to strangers and people who are better off as strangers? I don't. I've had to work through the regret of trusting those who were once my friends with intimate details and choices I made in my life, but it doesn't mean I need to continue allowing them access to it.

HOLLY'S HEALING TIP
Old friends aren't always good friends.
Time isn't a qualifier for quality.It's okay to let go of people who aren't nice to you
just because you've known them for a long time.

Are you thinking *it's easier to give in than fight?* If you are, that emotional truth needs healing. Because you are worth the fight, work, love, and tenderness. Healthy friendships do not require you to give until you feel empty or less-than. They shouldn't be a one-sided relationship.

How can you tell if your friend is a taker? Pay attention to how you feel when you leave them. Ask yourself if you're relieved to be away from them? Notice if you're fatigued. Do you feel anxious before you see them and worry about how it will go? Will they be nice or start in again?

What story do you tell yourself that makes it possible for you to stay even when your mind, body, and spirit give you signals that this person is not good for you? The anxiety and fatigue you feel are signals. They're telling you something isn't right. Pay attention to them. Your authentic self and intuition are trying to get your attention. Listen.

The giver and taker relationship is straightforward. The giver cares and demonstrates attachment by giving emotionally, spiritually, mentally, and physically, and the taker enjoys taking it all. The taker can be a narcissist or a person who is empty and looking for another person to heal their pain instead of taking charge of the healing process themselves. It's a process of paying attention to your honest feelings and the person you want to be.

A normal friendship includes a balance between give and take. There will be times when you are each other's sounding board, partner in crime, support, or truth-teller, and the relationship has room to grow and mature. Actual give and take to meet the friend where they are in life is a beautiful gift.

There's a familiar saying: friends are the family you choose. The power is in your hands.

HOLLY'S HEALING TIP
A friend is a person who is...
kind, considerate, takes time to check in, enjoys your company, seeks your input, tells you the truth even when speaking up is difficult, loves you, is honest, and wants the best for you.

There are differences among the ideas of knowing someone you don't like for a long time, knowing a person for a long time, and growing with them that are all important.

It's a gift to know someone over time despite periods of not talking to one another or being part of their everyday life. That requires love, patience, and acceptance.

A person can be a wonderful friend, even when they don't agree with your every decision or political view. It's good to hold space and not cut off or villainize a friend when they're frustrating you. It is okay to set a boundary and back away, but love can help heal.

If someone's beliefs don't align with my own, I don't care. I don't need friends to always agree with me or be an echo chamber. I have friends with whom I disagree. I don't share all of their political, emotional, or religious views. Having differences doesn't make someone an enemy. It makes them someone interesting to have conversations with. It means they have different perspectives. Those are good qualities. Only if and when a person demonizes or belittles me for not sharing similar beliefs do I put distance between us.

Remember, you're making room for the real you and friends who align with you. All you have to do is let go of those people who don't value and appreciate you.

Are virtual friends real?

The internet can be both a magical and dangerous place. Children are not the only ones who need to be reminded that people aren't always who they appear to be online. Catfishing happens. Predators of all kinds exist, as do pseudo friendships.

The virtual world has helped me to meet so many cool people from around the world. The internet also allows me to connect with people who may never have known about me, my writing, or my healing work. Like most things in this world, the internet is neither good nor bad, but rather gray. It's important to remember relationships carried out via screen aren't all genuine, and nothing can replace physical, intimate, human, face-to-face interaction.

There's a Twitter pitch contest called Pitch Wars. The contest helps writers connect with agents, publishers, and other writers. I entered years ago, and the Pitch Wars community was enjoyable, funny, and mostly full of writers supporting other writers. One woman, Mia, always posted things that made me laugh. Like me, she loved Halloween and had a GIF for everything.

Mia and I, along with another woman, Kimberly, began chatting online. Then we realized we lived relatively close to each other. We decided to meet in a neutral location. It was so fun to take that relationship offline and in person. Mia and Kimberly became real-world friends.

I joked, "You even look like your pictures!"

We've met for dinners and drinks for years now. We support each other through the publication journey, querying, getting agents, losing agents, publishing, and book promotion. Ours is a real friendship of like-minded writers. I think this is a rare and beautiful thing. Of course: use common sense if you do something like this! Please don't meet up with strangers you met online without someone else knowing who you're meeting, when you're meeting, and where you're meeting. Be smart!

For me, nothing replaces face-to-face communication. There is energy exchanged in those types of interactions that is different without a device between you.

A keyboard can't replace a touch or a smile. A screen can't hug you, tell you there's something between your teeth, clink your glass, or borrow your clothes — it is an inanimate object that can't smell, touch, or taste. Your senses are precious, so remember to feed them.

Although friendships can form on social media, you never really know if the other person is who they are presenting themselves to be. So please give the people who are real your time and attention. Be an active participant in your friendships.

Remember, friends don't make you feel bad or try to manipulate you. Friendship isn't based on doing favors for, coming to the rescue of, giving money to, agreeing one hundred percent with, having every single thing in common with, talking every day, or going along with things that make you feel uncomfortable, and they most definitely don't make you feel less-than.

Breathe that information in. Especially those people who like being needed and find fulfillment in helping others. There's a difference between kindness, being used, and hiding in behind being busy. If the need to help is so large, it's most likely a wound you're self-medicating, and it's a signal there is something more to heal. You may be repeating an unhealthy pattern. It's one with which you're familiar, but is it working for you, or is it leaving you feeling exhausted and on a never-ending treadmill of things to do and people to take care of?

What would happen if I asked you to slow down and experience that feeling? Sit with the discomfort and see what bubbles up. That's the place of healing, and maybe it's time to learn new ways of being.

Are your friends inconsiderate?

A client of mine is dealing with infertility. Her old friends lack empathy for her situation. They are cruel and catty. She tells me how unhappy she feels when she sees them, and in the same breath says she's known them her whole life and can't understand why they're not nicer.

"Maybe they've always been this way," I said.

My client looked at me, incredulously.

"Maybe they're who they've always been, and the relationships haven't matured while you have. Is that really what you want in your life? You never feel good after you see them."

She blinked at me. I gave her time to process what I said and how I felt about her situation.

"We can cut the cords to those friendships and ask that they reattach in a better way if you like."

"You're right," she said. "They haven't been supportive. We used to get together after work and talk over drinks. They had children when they were younger and can't understand me wanting to try having a family now."

"That has to be painful." In my heart, my clairvoyant and clairsentient gifts felt the grief she carried over her miscarriages, the fear she was masking of possibly never having a child, and her loneliness. She was outside of her friends' experiences. They said things like, "maybe next time," or "you can try again," and "at least it was early in the pregnancy." They didn't understand how those words belittled her experience and pain.

Well-meaning people may be the friends you need a little space from. It doesn't mean they aren't friends; it's just that they aren't the friends you need close. I told her, "We can set new boundaries and see what happens. Usually, when you set a boundary, you'll notice people are different with you. They'll either test the boundary, accept the boundary, or disappear because they know they can't mess with you anymore. The important thing is you won't be hurt, and you'll make room for supportive, kind friends to step in and love you."

HOLLY'S HEALING TIP
Set boundaries with friends.
When you set a boundary, you'll notice people may do
one of the following:
Test the boundary
Accept the boundary
Disappear because they know they can't mess with you

What is a boundary?

A boundary is an energetic line, letting the world know what you find acceptable and unacceptable. It's self-worth and protection. It's divine protection and an important part of self-care. But it isn't a wall or line drawn in the sand.

Be honest with where you are in your life, get real with yourself, and you'll stop making excuses for people hurting you.

What is an energy vampire?

Another important reason to create and maintain energetic boundaries with people is to keep vampires away. I'm not talking about the fictional characters many of us love. I'm talking about energy vampires — those individuals who sucks the life from you. Don't confuse them as friends. They are people who steal your energy, joy, and compassion, and then manipulate you to get what they want. I've never met a person who hasn't encountered at least one energy vampire in their lifetime.

A vampire can look like:

A person who needs to be the center of attention at all times.

A person who isn't satisfied until they get their own way.

A person who unloads or dumps all of their issues, problems, emotional baggage at your feet, and then walks away feeling better, leaving you feeling emotionally, spiritually, and mentally drained.

A person who only takes and never gives emotionally, spiritually, and mentally.

A person about whom your senses say, "Stay away from them."

I can see how a vampire literally connects energetic cords to their victim to control and siphon off their energy.

An energetic cord is not an illusion. It's something I see, like strings on a marionette from one person to another. Sometimes the cords are attached to a spot on the body, so the person has neck pain, lower back pain, or pain in the heart. These physical pains have energetic origins.

To heal, shift, and grow into the authentic you you're meant to be, you must be free of negative cords.

Let's eradicate the unhealthy connections between you and others, heal them, and create better ones.

What is a parent-child friendship?

In a parent-child friendship, one person demands, wants, needs a friend to take over an absent parent's role, while the other nurtures, holds space, and gives. In my experience, these roles are typically subconscious. Each individual has needs and wants the other can provide. Have you noticed I bring up needs and wants? For me, there is heat to a need. This means there is an emotional, mental, or spiritual wound attached to the need. There is a pain that wants soothing. It elicits over-the-top reactions. A want is a desire that can be communicated without dramatics.

81

HOLLY R. HUGHES

The person who is the child in the friendship will require emotional, mental, and at times, financial support. They will get mad when the parent in the relationship doesn't respond the way the child wants. The child in the relationship has a wound and is looking for you to heal it.

When I work with the parent in this type of friendship, we focus on healing the need to nurture. We explore the idea of taking on the role as a pattern of behavior they know and possibly do not like, or if it is a coping mechanism or a way to keep busy and not deal with healing their own issues.

The child in this type of friendship needs to heal differently. They have to reclaim their power. It's about trusting themselves, their judgment, and building confidence.

Do you like being a teacher or a student in a friendship?

The teacher likes to be the one in charge, control situations and get-togethers, and have some superiority or talent they want to show and teach you. If and when you learn the "lesson," this teacher will most likely exit your life and move onto teaching another. It can be a mutual outgrowing of each other or be done when the teacher feels threatened by the student learning more than they have to teach.

I've encountered this dynamic in friendships with other healers. I am drawn to certain people because I believe they can teach me things about my gifts, or possibly about gifts I don't possess, and the mentor-mentee relationship blooms into a friendship.

The snag happens when the student wants to be seen on their own as a unique voice. If the teacher is

82

threatened in any way by the student's capabilities or lack of need for their expertise, friendships can fizzle.

It can also manifest as a person who is a know-it-all, and some takers pose as students.

The best way to handle a student-teacher relationship is to give it time and space. If a new friendship based on mutual respect can't form because it's threatening or uncomfortable, then that friendship has run its course. Perhaps, in time, there can be a reconnection.

The key to healing friendships is letting go of expectations. Expectations are rarely voiced, and therefore, impossible to fulfill. Friends are a reflection of how you value and respect yourself. Nothing feels worse than spending time with people who don't understand, like, care for, and respect you. Personally, I don't share my time with people who aren't real and with whom I can't be genuine.

Holding onto unhealthy friendships is like having a clenched fist. You can't hold onto anything new. There is tension, pain, and fatigue. Intuitive energy healing can free you of the pain that no longer serves you. It's like me taking your clenched hand, giving you the ability to let go of the fist, and providing you the chance to relax.

I like to say it's not a matter of whether the cup is half empty or full, but rather how many you're holding and for how long.

I kept the focus of this chapter on friendship issues that need healing. But I want to take a moment and acknowledge the wonderful friends I have in my life. The person I've known since I was four, who grew up down the block from me, and lives states away now. I love the friends I've had for decades. The people who knew me and loved me when I was young and figuring things out, who supported me through my starter marriage and boyfriends, the career changes and the slap-the-table laughs. To the people I loved through the trials of life and who made mine richer for knowing them. I believe they feel the same way about me, and that is a wonderful feeling.

I adore the friends who did things with me that we never caught on tape and the people who came into my life recently. I love my dancing and writing friends. I don't need a large group to feel special. I cherish the diverse friendships in my life.

My cup is never half empty. It's full of room to grow. I have the people who get me, and I love them.

HOLLY'S HEALING HOMEWORK:

It's time to reach for your pen and paper again. Let's dig in and explore the friendships in your life and how they define you.

What kind of friend are you?

How many friends do you have?

How many of your friends are old friends?

With which friendship dynamic do you most identify?

Do you wonder how someone who's known you for so long can be dismissive or cruel?

Do you only hear from friends after you reach out?

Do these friends answer with one-word text messages?

Have you found out you're left out by seeing friends together on social media?

What do you expect from friendship?

Is there a need you have that you want a friend to fill?

What makes your friendships appealing?

What makes some of your friendships uncomfortable?

Do you make demands?

Do friends expect you to do things for them?

Are you still checking on what they're doing after you let go?

Do you have toxic friendships in your life now?

Do you surround yourself with people who talk about others behind their backs?

Do you feel better or worse after seeing friends?

Do your friends value you?

If your friends were a mirror into your self-worth, what does that mirror show?

Who are the people in your life to whom you need to say goodbye?

Who are the people in your life to whom you should hold on?

What kind of people did you create space for in your life?

How does exploring friendships make you feel?

Take time to answer all of the above questions and be honest. The goal is to create better relationships. Some friendships are worth fighting for, while others are better left in the past.

Friends don't require you to pay for friendships. There is no friend tax that mandates paying for things, doing favors for, taking on work, or any other demeaning tasks. Friendship should have a foundation of mutual respect, a shared interest, and a great level of care.

You may have fond and shared memories with people you outgrow. That's okay. Friendships evolve, as do the types of friends you want, especially when you embark on a healing journey. With awareness, change is possible. Take stock of what works, and let go of what and who no longer serves you.

Please do this with empathy for who you were, for who your friends were, and for where you're all headed. This simple meditation should help.

GUIDED MEDITATION

Read the meditation aloud. Get comfortable with the words, then record your voice saying it and play it back, or feel free to go to my website and listen to me saying it to you. Once you get the hang of meditating, please feel free to alter any words so they best align with you.

Here we go. Take a deep breath in and sigh it out. Breathe in trust and exhale anxiety. Breathe in peace and exhale chaos. Breathe in calm and exhale pain. Breathe in honesty and exhale lies. Breathe in self-worth and exhale insecurity. Breathe in love and exhale anger. I acknowledge the healing journey you are on, and I'm so proud of you for taking it. You are brave enough to know something in your life isn't working and taking the time to sort things out. All healing is done with love and light, compassion, and forgiveness.

I honor the spirit inside me.

I honor the loving spirits around me, both seen and unseen.

I release every energy that does not serve me.

I free myself from connections to people in my past who have hurt me.

I let go of what was and make room for what is and will be.

I ask that any relationship that isn't for my highest good end.

I forgive myself for allowing friends to hurt me.

I forgive myself for being hurt.

I ask that the wounds on my heart and soul be healed.

I release myself from the karmic contract and unhealthy friendship patterns I've known, and welcome new friends and love into my life.

91

I accept my role and ask to learn how to be a better friend.

I will learn how to receive friendship.

Take another deep breath in, and exhale any grief. Imagine your body floating a few feet above the ground. You are at ease and comfortable. Imagine opening your eyes as you float. Look down to see if there are any cords connected to you. They may appear as chains, ropes, cords of light, or sound. They may be thick or thin. We are going to cut all of the friendship cords that no longer serve you. Feel free to call upon an angel to help you with this work. Archangel Raziel is available to assist you with this task. Archangel Raziel is known as "The Secret of God." He is known to have spiritual insights meant for you, directly from God.

Imagine Raziel holding a divine pair of scissors and gently cutting the energy cord. Then see in your mind's eye the piece of cord that is cut, but still attached to you, dissolve. If there is a mark on your ethereal body, we ask that Mary Magdalene and Raziel heal it.

I want you to imagine a shimmering gold salve being placed over the wounds. Know that the balm is love and light, that it's meant for you, and that you deserve the healing. You are being supported and loved throughout this process.

Release expectations and preconceived notions of what this clearing meditation feels like. If you have difficulty imagining the things I am saying, it's okay. You don't have to see it to receive the healing. If you're not ready to let go of a friendship, you may ask that the cord between you and that specific friend reattach in a healthy way.

I ask that these cord cuttings be done in the highest intention, with love.

I call back any energy I have given away, knowingly or unknowingly, and ask that it be cleared in God's heavenly light before it's returned to me.

Now I want you to close your eyes and imagine the most beautiful rain filling up a sacred pool of water. Then I want you to walk into the warm water and float. You should feel relaxed and at ease, knowing you are receiving divine love and protection. Imagine all of the energy you gave away throughout your life coming back to you. It seeps into your skin, moves into your bloodstream, fills your muscles and organs, and calms your thoughts and emotions. You feel safe and whole.

I honor God all around me. I see God as an energetic boundary surrounding you in shimmering golden light. It encircles your whole being, starting three feet below your feet, all-around your outstretched arms, and closes two feet above your head. Inside this boundary is your soul's sacred space. It is clear of pain, anxiety, loss, grief, and uncertainty. It's here to remind you of your connection to God and is available to you any time you want to feel it.

I always end my meditations by saying, "Thank you," or "Amen."

Slowly open your eyes and look around you. Take notice of how you feel. What's changed? Write it down, so when you're feeling uncertain about friends, you can come back to this meditation and remind yourself how worthwhile it is to take the time to quiet your mind and ask for help cutting unhealthy cords.

Six

What are your family values and pathology?

I saved talking about family for the halfway point. I wanted to make sure you settled into your heart and feelings before tackling this incendiary topic. Family dynamics tend to be complicated. I know mine are. Remember to be honest and kind — heap forgiveness onto yourself for how you handled things. I'm sure you did your best. Please consider settling into a comfortable spot, wrap yourself in a soft blanket, and enjoy a cup of tea before you begin to excavate this part of your story.

Unpacking family pathology is a crucial step in becoming the real, happy you. To move on from your past, and heal this transition point, ask yourself what traits you have inherited from your family? It's a hot topic and one that's best taken one emotional truth at a time. I know you have the strength and ability to face and heal the issues that arise.

You only know what you are taught. Your family not only taught you with words, but they communicated non-verbally, too. In my experience with clients, people learn more from non-verbal familial messages than verbal ones.

Here are patterns I've seen in familial pathology:

Denial
Abuse
Belittling
Choosing partners who perpetuate family dynamics
Not finishing things
Erratic emotional behavior
Victim mentality
Work ethic
Degrading another
Lying
The parent making the child feel less-than

People come into my office and share their family stories with me. Sometimes, they spend the entire session venting their anger about how someone did them wrong. They blame a parent or sibling for their emotional turmoil, and they don't stop repeating the story. I call this being stuck in a groove. Think of a record player back in the day, and the needle has fuzz on it and is skipping in a single groove of the record.

The popular vernacular for this mindset is "victim mentality." People believe they're at the mercy of everything that happened to them, and other people are to blame for their problems.

Whatever personal chaos is going on, the mess you learned from growing up in the household you did doesn't need to define you for the rest of your life. The behavior is learned, but it can be reversed. You just have to be willing to let it go and welcome in something new.

Stop blaming, and start changing. I believe you are capable of healing the painful familial patterns and the emotional wounds that haunt you.

HOLLY'S HEALING TIP
You can always change habits, forgive, and heal.

When I write about my parents, I always feel guilty about painting them in time one way or another for you to judge. I love my parents. They did so many things right in bringing me up: they loved and supported me, and yes, there are instances when they made mistakes. When I share, I am not laying my life experiences out for you to think horrible thoughts about — I don't want that. I share my experience so you will appreciate that my empathy comes from personal understandings and not only the insights I receive intuitively.

One of the most complicated love entanglements I have is with my father. My father is an alcoholic. Growing up in our house was full of challenges that, to this day, confound my mind because they're my normal, and they're unpleasant.

My father came home angry every night I lived at home. He'd walk into the house raging about how an employee did him wrong or how a company wanted the impossible. It didn't matter what the cause of his anger was. His rage filled the house with a smell and energy that scared me. He moved fast, and he would run his fingers through his hair, flick his thumbnail on his top front teeth as a sign for *fuck you,* yell at my mother as if she was the cause, all as his way of venting. In hindsight, I understand he had to have been drunk when he did these things. I know this because I saw the rage bubble up at family parties or dinners out. Alcohol + Dad = RAGE.

When I say rage, I know you can't imagine exactly what it was like. It's hard for me to tell you, and I lived through it. The closest thing is to imagine a tornado

97

whipping shrapnel at your face, while a butter knife stabs through your ribs to pierce your heart, and a window to hell opens, forcing you to stare into your worst fears all at once.

One of my defense mechanisms is to disassociate. My father's anger flew from his body with such force, I had no other option than to hide both physically and emotionally. My husband witnessed this behavior in my thirties, and he picked me up and removed me from the room.

My husband, then-boyfriend, asked me, "Where did you go? It was like you went catatonic."

I didn't have an answer.

I was shaking in fear and embarrassment. What man could love a woman who had a parent like that? Who would choose to open themselves to such madness? His expression forced me to admit how often my father behaved horrendously. I had to remember.

I think that's when I labeled the drunk version of my parental unit as my father, and I labeled the sober one my dad. You'd think I would've gone to Al-Anon, but I didn't. There was something too raw in saying any of this out loud. It was safe on paper, in a journal, or appearing in my work. But I didn't know how to tell people who don't know what it's like how being loved by an addict changes the marrow of your spirit.

My father never addressed or acknowledged his violent outbursts the morning after. He'd wake up and pretend it never happened. One of the most painful things he did while an active alcoholic was leaving my wedding without saying anything to me. He left the reception, and a cousin told me my father was furious because he wasn't getting enough attention. My father also bailed on the family breakfast the next morning by unexpectedly renting a car and driving seventy-one miles to Palm Springs without word of where he had gone. He did the convenient amnesia routine when I heard from him days later. He didn't remember leaving, and he didn't remember I had planned an outing for the following day. For a while he ruined all the good memories from the day with his alcoholic cruelty. I had to get myself to the place where his bad behavior no longer defined or limited my experiences.

The pathology I suffered from was ignoring abusive behavior because I knew he loved me. I was taught to ignore his outbursts no matter who he attacked. As an empath and his look-alike daughter, I absorbed his pain and rage and twisted it to form the belief that it was my responsibility to make him happy. It was my job to never invoke his temper. The onus was on me to make him smile.

My father said the cruelest, horrible, most shocking things when drunk. He called me by the wrong name, yelled at me for doing something when I lived across the country and wasn't even there to have done it, cursed at me, and reminisced about childhood memories as if we were back in time.

He tore people down and belittled them. He scared me more times than I can count or remember. I had to create a way to disappear to take on all of his emotionally festering wounds.

Recognizing the pattern I was recreating was one step in my healing. Understanding that my normal wasn't normal took time. I didn't feel comfortable if there wasn't tension, and I simultaneously hated the tension. I did the healing work and learned I could create home the way that best suited me. Now my definition of home and family includes emotional, creative, physical, and mental safety and wellness.

What did growing up in your house teach you?

I have no idea what goes on behind closed doors until someone comes to see me. One shared family dynamic is to cover up. Are there things that are your normal, but you hate? You may not be aware of how you define yourself in terms of what your family did to you. You could be stuck in a groove, and I want to help you climb out of it.

I see many people who, as children, were used as a tool to inflict emotional and financial pain. The children become objects or instruments instead of humans to grow and nourish.

Other clients want to be loved, but they have difficulty receiving the love they crave because being vulnerable wasn't part of what made them feel safe in their family dynamic. They're so used to and conditioned to brace for negative interactions that it's challenging to process or accept when good things come into their life. These clients end up self-sabotaging the good thing and recreate a dynamic they know, despite being unhappy with it.

The family pathology I learned from my parents was:

Love a broken person and subjugate yourself to their will to demonstrate love.

Do everything you can to make peace.

Deny your feelings or pain and fear to assuage the feelings of others.

This is a pattern I repeated in all of my relationships until it nearly disintegrated me.

I had no understanding or ownership of my familial pathology until I was deeply unhappy in my starter marriage. I married an emotionally and mentally abusive man. I believed *if I love him enough, I can make him happy.*

This is a lie.

I met him on a movie set a few months after I moved to Los Angeles. He was the art director, and I was a production assistant. I first noticed him when he was sitting in the production office on location reading the same book I was reading. He was seven years older than I was, and I equated him with more talent, smarts, and life experience. We started talking and flirting. When production wrapped, my roommates and I had a party. I invited him, but I never imagined he'd come. He arrived wearing a black leather fringe coat, and he looked out of place in our North Hollywood, early twenty-something party.

I told him I had a boyfriend. He responded, "When you know what you want, call me." Then he left.

We were dating by the end of the week. I learned how the divorce from his first wife was nearly final. He told me how she'd wronged him. His pain resonated with me. I felt terrible for him. I couldn't believe a wife could take off the ring he gave her to escape their marriage.

He was tall and thin. My only criteria for being in the relationship was I had to fit into his pants. I told myself if I'm skinny enough to wear his jeans, I'll stay. They fit. I stayed. We moved in together within a month.

He said, "I'll love you as long as you don't gain any weight." He said my shoes were ugly. He told me to work harder when he remained unemployed for months on end. I worked hard so he could write a full script with a friend. He berated me for not making dinner, not having the laundry done, everything he was upset I wasn't doing. He stayed home but didn't work on his writing. Instead, he watched television and did nothing else. My insides told me I must work harder to make him happy. His behavior became worse and worse. Before long, I married him. I knew this kind of man. His pain was my standard. I saw my mother take abuse. I knew I could do it, too.

I thought I was strong, but really, I was messed up. I hated the situation I had created and found myself in, but it was what I knew. I was stuck and unhappy.

HOLLY'S HEALING TIP
Sometimes your unhappiness
comes from being stuck in what you know,
but it no longer serves you.

The magical, spiritual intervening moment in my life happened at work. I was producing my first episode of an HBO series, and the art director pulled me aside.

I remember her long dark hair and don't recall liking her very much. "Do you know you cry every day at three o'clock?" she asked. Her eyes were dark and kind, but somehow they made me uneasy.

"No," I said. I thought she was crazy.

"You do. You cry every day at three. Here," she handed me a card. It was for her therapist. She said she was terrific. That day at three o'clock, I became aware of the tears I was shedding. My mirror moment could no longer be denied. I literally saw I was crying and was so wholly dissociative I wouldn't have believed it unless my reflection forced me to see my anguish. A stranger knew I needed help better than I did, and it forced me to face my truth.

The art director's insight and bravery to talk to me so honestly was what I consider divine intervention. I called the therapist, and my healing journey began.

My therapist was a lifeline. When I began therapy, I didn't know my father was an alcoholic. I didn't think he was drunk. It took going back to my journals to recognize the truth. The journals said over and over, year after year, "Dad's drunk. Dad came home drunk. Dad's drunk and angry."

I remember reading that and feeling shock burn through me. My disassociated mind smacked up against emotional truth. I was the daughter of an alcoholic, which affected my judgment, emotional maturity, and well-being. It influenced how I made friends and the kinds of people I invited into my life. I was emotionally enmeshed in my nuclear family dynamics, and my sense of well-being was connected to the trauma and drama in my life.

How do you act around your family?

My husband used to tell me I was one version of myself around my parents and another everywhere else. It pissed me off. He saw my blind spot and called me out on it. I didn't like it. He said it shortly after he carried me out of the room in which my father was raging.

Can you relate? Are you one version of yourself at home with family and another outside of their presence? I'm not talking about respecting traditions. I want to know if you lose your voice, your shine, your thoughts, your opinions, and your sense of self around them. Do you bottle it all up because the battle to be real is too much?

If you notice yourself pretending to get along, then there's work to be done. This also may be a blind spot for you, as it was for me.

I bet your body, spirit, and guides are trying to get your attention. Anxiety and fatigue before, during, and after a family visit are signals. They are a physical response to a pain point in your life. And I'm not talking about rolling your eyes at hearing the same stories you heard growing up or when a cousin makes a bad joke. I'm asking you to be honest about the knot you twist into and how you behave around your parents and siblings.

To never add to the emotional turmoil in my home, I kept secrets, and I tried to control every circumstance and situation in my life.

My friends had emotional baggage, too. The pain in me recognized their pain, and we collided. My job was to help people. I picked not such great people and invited them into my life. Over and over, they hurt and disappointed me. I became what I had learned non-verbally at home.

My family pathology was to cover up, make nice, look good, be smart, not say anything to anyone, keep secrets, do well, overachieve, cover up, be numb, be kind, work hard, push past the pain, ignore my hurt, and look happy all the while.

I got to a place in my life where what I knew was no longer working for me. I had to change habits, forgive myself and my family, and then heal.

What are your family patterns?

Healing happens from the inside out. You'll never be thin enough, contoured enough, or rich enough to earn happiness. Look at all of the famous, wealthy people who are miserable.

Blame, shame, and guilt are honest feelings, but holding onto them only leads to chaos. Together we can work through them and heal them so you can be free and happy. We will establish energetic boundaries so you stop feeling responsible for your family's well-being. Instead of being a mosaic of reactions, you can create your own energetic self-portrait.

HOLLY'S HEALING TIP
You don't have to stop being you
to let go of unhealthy patterns.

Breaking unhealthy patterns and stepping away from family pathology requires work. You must be willing to dig into your heart and feel vulnerable. Expect the need for a box of tissues, fuzzy socks, and a blank journal as your tools for self-discovery and healing. It's about unearthing the things you do, owning your behavior, and admitting and honoring that you've done the best you know.

One exercise I use for this is writing forgiving statements. I ask you to write them out longhand. The statements all begin with: I forgive myself for... Then, you fill in the blanks.

Some examples are:

I forgive myself for ignoring what I knew hurt me.

I forgive myself for becoming what I hate.

I forgive myself for hurting the people I love.

I forgive myself for forgetting to take care of myself.

I forgive myself for ignoring the pain for so long that it changed me.

Please try to keep empathy in your heart while you do this exercise.

Add in love and kindness for you and the people from whom you learned. People may have hurt you, but I bet they probably did the best they knew how. They may be struggling with the same pathology and never took the time to heal the wounds they suffered at the hands of a family pathos. Own and honor that you recognize the pattern that no longer serves you. Understand it took a lifetime to learn it, and it will require time, patience, and practice to unlearn it. It may take emotional upheaval to stop being triggered or reactionary. Forgiveness and desire to learn a new way of being is all you need now. Congratulate yourself for taking a big first step.

When you let go of what doesn't work for you, you create space for what does.

Remember, time is not the enemy, but rather a tool in your arsenal. Healing is not an overnight juice cleanse that eliminates the waste stored in your body. The fact is that healing has layers. This is part of an onion peel that you're stripping away, and it's a vulnerable place to be. Be kind to yourself. Eat good food. Stay sober. Get plenty of sleep. Take Epsom salt baths. Go for walks in nature. Don't push away the feelings or memories that come up, but rather greet them, as they are the story that needs healing.

Are you a person who has done their work, and yet you find yourself still repeating a pattern? There are a few reasons why this may be the case. The first reason is, even for those of us who do our spiritual work, that damn onion has many layers, and relationships trigger us, then we have to go back and deal with the deeper level of trauma and our stories.

Some people fake doing the work. They watch lots of online videos, quote self-help books, seek out healers and teachers, but they don't implement what they learn. Those people often like to tell others what's wrong in their lives. They give advice instead of empathy and don't walk their talk. Fixing other people's problems is more comfortable than managing their own mess. They come across as self-righteous and bossy.

There are no shortcuts to being brave and changing what isn't working. The work is simple and can be terrifying. That's encouraging and not at all scary, right? You have to own your shit. You have to be able to identify what's not working for you and decide no matter what, you're going to find a way to let go of the pattern and pathology, and create a new way of being, coping, managing, and living. Happiness is an option.

What about depression?

I'd like to take a moment to address depression. In my experience as an intuitive healer, I'm not able to move the energy of depression out or away from a person. When clients come in depressed, I feel it as pressure and a headache on the left side of my forehead. This is when it's vital to be treated by a professional who can prescribe medication. Medication is a wonderful tool and must be administered by a doctor. Please don't self-medicate.

I know what being depressed feels like for me. Several years ago, I had a hysterectomy, and the recovery was much more painful than I imagined.

To make matters worse, my intuitive abilities disappeared. When I stopped to think about it, it made sense. My uterus was removed, along with a huge fibroid that grew inside it, and when it was cut out, my second chakra was removed along with it.

My inner world fell silent. The feelings and insights that were a natural part of my every day and moment were suddenly quiet. I wondered, *Is this is how everyone else feels?* It was a lonely place for me to be in. Stuck in bed, in incredible post-op pain, my spiritual support vanished. I missed hearing my guides and the sensory connection to everything we can't see, but which we feel. Most of all, I missed the invisible support and peacefulness that came with meditation and connection.

A month went by, and my grief melted into the cells of my body. Gravity was stronger, and my limbs weaker. I wanted to lie down, cry, and keep a blanket over my head. Simple tasks took a Herculean effort.

I had an awareness of my downward spiral, so I made sure to eat right, I made myself go to exercise classes, didn't drink alcohol, yet I still felt awful. I called my doctor and told him what was going on with me. He prescribed an anti-depressant.

He said, "This is to help you get over the hump. It won't be forever. After three months, see how you feel, and if you feel better, you can stop."

My doctor was right. I only took the anti-depressant for a few months and was able to transition off of it. Please, make sure you are honest with your doctors and have them monitor dosage. Sometimes dosage needs to be changed, or a different medicine needs to be prescribed. I am not a healthcare professional. Trust your doctor. If you don't understand what they recommend, ask questions, advocate for your health, but don't play the *I looked it up on the internet, and this should work for me* game. You're worth the time and energy to go to the doctor. Okay?

I believe a person needs support to make a change. It's exceedingly difficult to read a manual, and expect the person can stop doing what they always did in order to start doing something new.

This is where my practice comes in. I support you through the transitions and help navigate the emotional process of change. I help you connect to the love and support around you that you can't see or feel, and then I help you feel it. When I meditate and think of you, and especially when I am talking with you, my guides connect to yours. My body will flood with emotional information, and I will simply know things I can't possibly know. I use all of the skills and gifts I spoke about at the beginning of the book.

Your guides will help me navigate your emotional truths and assist your healing when you can't articulate the hurt. Since I have no emotional triggers connected to your family, I can sidestep what makes moving past patterns and pain difficult for you.

People with painful secrets always ask, "How do you know that?"

I know it because part of you wants to let go and heal, and allowing me into your energetic soul space will facilitate that growth and recovery. Trusting me to experience you at your most vulnerable lets me see the energy (chords, connections, emotions, light beings, guides, spiritual masters, angels, trauma) around you and connected to you.

I believe a big part of cutting the cords that link you to family pathology includes surrender, forgiveness, and imagination. It's vital to forgive yourself for what's happened and imagine how wonderful it will be when (insert what you want here).

What's the thing that drives you crazy about your family, the thing that is the most self-destructive, self-sabotaging, unfulfilling thing *you're* doing? Where are you an echo instead of an individual?

HOLLY'S HEALING TIP
Be an original, not a copy.

Your goal in life should be to remain authentic and real, not perfect. Not what others want you to be. You can change any patterns you want. It only takes trusting the process and letting go of what no longer works. A new system will meet you and carry you forward.

Owning your self-worth and managing self-care doesn't have to equate to cutting yourself off from your family. Who they are doesn't define you. When you untangle your worth from their definitions, you'll be able to set realistic expectations of their behavior and create plans to navigate the relationships. This can be as simple as limiting the time you spend together, not discussing hot topics, and walking away from a situation instead of engaging in it.

Hold space for them to be who they are, and more importantly, hold space for what is true for you. Your truth matters. Being vulnerable doesn't make you weak; it makes you a warrior.

This is the space to acknowledge the former blind spots in your family dynamics and heal them. If your family is not safe for you, that's a different situation. I'm focused on helping you discover who you are versus what your family says, thinks, and pressures you to be.

HOLLY'S HEALING HOMEWORK:

Write down the dynamics inside the home you grew up in:

List what you hated about the house you grew up in:

What did you love about the home you grew up in?

What patterns of behavior did you emulate?

How did your family make you strong?

What patterns do you perpetuate even though you never liked them?

What pattern(s) of behavior are you ready to let go of?

Who are you ready to forgive?

GUIDED MEDITATION

Get in a comfortable position. It can be sitting in a favorite chair or lying on your back. All that matters is your comfort. When you're settled in, read these words aloud.

I honor the spirit inside me.

I honor the loving spirits around me, both seen and unseen.

I remove any energy that is not mine and which does not belong to me and return it to its owner. If they can't handle it, I ask that it be held in a safe place until they can.

Here I want you to visualize the family dynamic you no longer wish to replicate. I want the story that you believe was taught by your family to be released. Imagine letting go of a rope tied around your waist or a heavy book clutched to your chest. You should immediately feel lighter and better. That story is over. We're creating space for a new, better one. Who you are and who you want to become is enough. You are loved. You aren't responsible for the actions of others.

Let yourself appreciate this emerging you. The you who you want to be — the one who doesn't let the past define them, and who is brave, loving, creative, kind, and healthy.

I call back any energy I hid away and ask that it be cleansed in God's heavenly light and returned to me.

Take a deep breath in. What color do you see? What sensation do you feel as you exhale? That is your energy color today.

Allow that energy to sink into your body as a light coming from heaven down through the crown chakra on the very top of your head. It fills your mind, moves into your throat, freeing your voice and the things you never said, then heads into your heart, shoulders, and arms. You can feel it fill your fingertips. The light fills up your torso, giving you strength and energy. It moves past your hips and down your legs, through your thighs, past your knees, and into your shins, calves, and your feet until you feel a tingle in your toes.

Take a breath and feel how calling your energy back makes you feel whole and healthier. Then, say the words:

I cut the cords between me and my (mother, father, brother, sister, family) and ask that they reattach in a healthy way. I ask for support from Archangel Ezekiel, a high vibration angel that helps people experience true forgiveness. He leads people to joy and spiritual freedom. He helps free them from judgmental behavior and the unwillingness to forgive, helping them move past troubling memories as a means of alleviating painful emotions.

I forgive myself for living in a pain-filled space when the world wants to share its beauty and love. I deserve to honor and receive this love.

I won't use the past to punish myself any longer. I won't use it to hurt me or my family. From this moment on, I will step away from the darkness that is my familial emotional pain and accept Ezekiel's hand, as he wants to lead me into my happiness. I am open to creating a new definition of family. I am open to love.

When you have said these words, find a sound that will reinforce this. It can be a chime, a crystal bowl tone, a bell, a bird chirp, or a favorite song. When you hear this sound, it will reinforce your healing. It will connect you to this particular moment of healing so you will always have access to it.

Then honor God all around you. Imagine God as a beautiful, gold-flecked light that encircles you. The circle starts three feet below your feet and reaches wide enough to encompass your outstretched arms and close three feet above your head.

Inside this golden bubble is unconditional love and light. It is a boundary. It is a safe place for you to reconnect to your highest self, self-worth, and feelings. From this place of love, set your intention to heal. Set your intention to forgive. And set your intention to love yourself unconditionally.

What once held me back is gone. I am free.

When you feel ready, and there is no rush, end the meditation by saying, "Amen."

Write the thoughts and feelings that come to you during this meditation in your journal. Honor your subconscious and spiritual mind and body for knowing the healing you need in the given moment. Listen to what your body says. Hear your own highest self, that inner guide, leading you toward happiness. You deserve happiness.

For the rest of the day, I want you to eat very healthy food. Cut out junk food out for the next few days. Treat your body kindly. Take a salt bath and, at the very least, use salt scrub in the shower. I highly recommend using a eucalyptus spray or sage to clear your house. Finish releasing the toxic energy pattern you once lived with and make room for love and happiness.

Seven

Why is it so hard to forgive?

Forgiveness is a juggernaut. It's hard because it is an evolution. It's a blooming peony, with layers of soft, fragile petals that yearn to be open, but run the risk of being hurt when they do. Forgiveness is about trusting how you feel, honoring your truth, and setting yourself free from the pain. It is not about forgetting how another person treated you.

HOLLY'S HEALING TIP
Forgiveness is part of our evolution.

Maturing from infant to child to teenager, on to young adult, and into adulthood is about metamorphosis, as is your spiritual growth. We experience striving, lust, dream, creation, desire, and a host of other emotions designed to help us mature.

Being stagnant isn't natural to the human condition. Holding grudges, no matter how justified they feel, doesn't serve us. When we choose not to heal and forgive, I believe it leads to unhappiness, bitterness, loss of friendship and kindness, and, ultimately, illness. See, forgiving is never about the person who hurt you. It's about you.

Our spiritual well-being is meant to progress. Think of it as an evolution of your being. You are made of a mind, body, and the spiritual elements of your soul. I believe we choose to come to Earth and are meant to learn lessons. Our soul wants to experience the universe through human sensory perception. Through our trials and tribulations in life, we have the opportunity to learn from our mistakes and encounters, and evolve. Each person has a unique life journey.

I believe those who do not step up and learn from their pasts are more unhappy than those of us who try and succeed, or try and fail spectacularly.

Forgiveness is woven into the fabric of our time here on the planet. I've never met a person who did not experience the need to forgive or be forgiven in their life.

Forgiveness is not one note. Let's create an orchestra. This is what that means. There are times in my life when I think I am one hundred percent sure I'm over a loss or emotional pain. I wholeheartedly believe it, and then something in life happens, and the wound reappears – swollen, bloody, and painful.

When it reappears, I have to acknowledge it and heal it at a deeper level. This is especially true with forgiveness. People tend to push your buttons, and although you may be able to rise above or maintain a healthy boundary, sometimes you get triggered and hurt despite it all.

Where does forgiveness start?

Forgiveness starts with you. If you can't forgive yourself, how will you forgive others? One of the reasons our planet and humanity are suffering from so much chaos, prejudice, judgments, and divisiveness is because we haven't healed our personal shit, and it's being reflected onto us. All of our emotional pain is set loose upon the world like Pandora's box has been opened. It's time to take back our individual monsters and heal them.

We start the forgiveness journey close to home with you. Together, we'll let go of negative self-talk and make room for the real you. When you are kinder to yourself, the hope is that you will be more considerate of others. We start with you, because if you can't forgive yourself, how can you expect to forgive others?

Clients come to me to free themselves from the emotional chains and scars created by entanglements. These include relationships with narcissists, abusers, and people who placed unsaid expectations on these clients, leaving wounds on their self-worth. But those stories are too personal to share, and I want to begin more simply. I want to demonstrate how the smallest voice inside my own head did so much damage.

HOLLY'S HEALING TIP
Forgive yourself for believing other people's descriptions
of you. Define yourself with your own words.

I used to think I was meant to be in the background. I always wanted to be successful, but I wanted to be the person behind the person. I told myself other people had more talent.

Back in the day when I worked in film and television production in Los Angeles, I surrounded myself with super creative and talented people. I admired their imagination and couldn't see, claim, or recognize my own imaginative gifts. I lived with artists and writers and only dreamed about one day producing something.

My inner voice told me I wasn't creative enough. I was a problem solver. So, to remain around creative people, I did what I thought made me indispensable. I solved other people's issues, made their creative dreams come true, hired crew, negotiated contracts, worked with the Screen Actors Guild, the Directors Guild, and the Producers Guild of America. I had contacts with location services and rental houses. If production needed something, from expendables to extras, I knew who to call to make what we needed appear. I created budgets, yet not an ounce of my creativity was seen. When I shared ideas for making a scene work, including what to do with hair, makeup, locations, set design, or the script, my thoughts were absorbed, but I never received credit. My negative inner voice didn't allow me to fight for the acknowledgment I deserved.

Eventually, these feelings made me angry. I didn't want to be a line producer; I wanted to be a creative producer. But people had put me in a box, and I didn't see any opportunity to make that shift. The people I worked for didn't want to lose me as an asset. They also didn't want to pay me my worth or give me credit for my work to help me move up the ladder.

I was too good at being small and working hard. It was then that I learned I had to wave my arms and make noise about myself. I had to risk it all to find my voice and own my worth. I needed to shut that self-doubt monster up and stop believing it when it told me I wasn't enough. It meant walking away from what wasn't working. It was scary, and I was honestly bitter. I spent countless hours and years building a career that didn't want me.

For me, there was no success worth the abusive nature of film and television production. My subconscious mind sought and found an industry that re-created my family's emotional and physical turmoil and stress. It's what I knew, and even though I didn't like it, I was comfortable in it. The thing is, at twenty-eight, I was no longer willing to play the game or be part of the system as I knew it. I had to change radically.

I had to remember my love of writing that I'd had since I was a child, then relearn how to write, and be creative in a way that benefited no one other than myself. I had to find my voice.

HOLLY'S HEALING TIP
Don't silence your voice.
Set it free, and listen to it sing.

This meant starting at the beginning. I understood I needed help and decided to take classes at UCLA extensions. I was a beginner with an expert's heart. My work was rough at best, but I kept at it and didn't quit when I heard others read their work aloud and felt like I had a million miles to go to ever catch up. I signed up for more classes with different teachers, and I kept writing. I studied short stories, personal essays, and memoirs. I went on writing retreats in France, sat in workshops, drafted, and revised. My imagination returned. It was magical, and I ultimately found my voice. It was lyrical and emotional, and it was one hundred percent mine. My first drafts were full of sentences written in a way Yoda would be proud of, but not a single editor can print. My worst writing habit is switching tenses in a story and not being able to see that I've done it when I read it on my screen.

The point is it didn't matter how good or bad I was at writing. Ignoring and silencing part of my soul was self-inflicted cruelty.

Instead of surrounding myself with creative people, I became the creative individual I've always been. My artistic circle of friends champions one another. My work is published. An essay of mine went viral. I have a literary agent, and I've written three books. This was a huge turning point in my life.

HOLLY'S HEALING TIP
Stop surrounding yourself with what you like, and instead, work to become it.

I forgave myself for thinking I was meant to be in the background. I stepped into my big girl, thigh-high boots and took a step toward authenticity. I had to be okay with not being the best in the room, and I had to start owning when I was. Because if I don't believe in my talent, why should anyone else?

There is no cosmic law that dictates that your passion must be the same as your career. Sometimes, work is work. And the things you love to do, like curling, or sewing, are hobbies. The act of doing what you enjoy energizes you and connects you to a source of divine love that only wants the best for you. It wants you to engage in what makes you happy, as long as that doesn't hurt anyone or anything.

Forgive yourself for believing the definitions that belittle you. Forgive yourself for ignoring your dreams, wishes, wants, and curiosities, and try doing them now.

Own who you are now and dare to imagine who you will be. When you free yourself from self-punishment, you'll be whole with a new perspective. You'll be the real, happy you.

Can one sentence really have an impact?

Yes! A single declarative statement of forgiveness is massively healing. Use this as a template:

I forgive myself for judging myself as (unlovable, deniable, forgettable, stupid, slow, less-than, unworthy, ugly, quiet, boring, lacking talent, invisible).

Then, I want you to go to the mirror and say it to yourself. Forgive yourself. Look into your beautiful eyes and repeat it. Record the same message on your phone and play it back daily.

We value uniqueness in snowflakes, so let's use the same standard for people. We are all different, and the differences are beautiful.

This simple request may make you incredibly uncomfortable. I understand it's another one of Pandora's unboxed monsters. I'm an expert at picking myself apart. I can all too quickly tell you what I see as my flaws. For much too much of my life, I saw my flaws first. We must retrain ourselves to recognize our beauty instead of our perceived and socially conditioned flaws.

HOLLY'S HEALING TIP
Look in the mirror now and find one thing you like.
Retrain your eyes and mind to see your individual beauty
instead of your perceived and socially conditioned flaws.

Don't believe me when I say I'm an expert self-flaw finder? Here are a few I'm always personally working on overcoming: I'm too hairy. I have moles on my face. The skin on my neck sags.

Did you notice the things I negate myself with are superficial and about my body? Who's to blame for that?

The media? Models? The fashion and beauty industries? Celebrity culture? Instagram filters? Vanity?

Growing up, I always felt as though I was less than every blonde girl. I felt this with every fiber of my being. Boys like blonde girls better than girls with dark hair and eyes. It's ridiculous when I see it written out now, realizing how many years I spent devaluing myself because of some false belief. The question, however, is why I had that belief?

Maybe it was because my ninth-grade boyfriend broke up with me on Valentine's Day to be with a blonde. Or that many boyfriends broke up with me to date blondes. I can feel the old, useless anger boil up inside my chest now, just remembering that feeling.

I should forgive myself for doing so much emotional harm to myself.

I forgive myself for ever believing I was less valuable because I had brown hair. I forgive myself for comparing myself to other girls and hurting myself in the process. I forgive myself for being jealous of blondes. I forgive myself for thinking I ever had to be something other than myself to be worthy of love. I forgive myself for thinking I'm not desirable.

Instead of looking outside ourselves, forgiveness must come from within. The best person to forgive and make amends with first is yourself.

What are the qualities you like about yourself? I love my quirkiness. I like my fashion sense. I love my taste in music, art, and dance. I love reading. I want to learn. I like how I love. I like how I care about others. Did you notice I didn't write anything vain down? The things I name that I love about myself aren't defined by physical features. There are things about my physical appearance

I like. I love my eyebrows. I have a cool belly button. I have strong legs and an hourglass curve in my waist. I have pretty and healthy hair on my head and strong nails. I like my smile, and I think it's cool how my hazel eyes have every other eye color, except blue, mixed in them.

I used to spend time wishing I was thinner, that my thighs wouldn't touch, that my butt was smaller, and I used to want to be three inches taller. It's incredible the number of hours I spent hurting myself with all of my negative self-worth beliefs. When I step back from that truth, I can see that I've mentally and spiritually abused my self-worth for years.

Negative self-talk is normalized in our culture. Ads are incessantly telling us what we need to make ourselves better. Be brave. Dare to love yourself despite the world telling you different.

Go into your journal and write what you *like* about yourself. Be honest. Be courageous and vulnerable. Own it. Celebrate all of the things that make you who you are.

HOLLY'S HEALING TIP
Forgive yourself for belittling your talent, intelligence, worth, beauty, and heart.

How do I forgive those who hurt me?

This is the million-dollar question. There are so many kinds of hurt. The hurt after a breakup. The pain of neglect. The agony of abuse. The crazy-making pain after you realize you've been used or manipulated.

For me, forgiveness is about you. Holding on to hate and fury can erode a person from the inside out.

Earlier I shared that I'm the adult daughter of an alcoholic. I lived through lies, emotional and mental battering, and his rage. My father is also wicked smart, generous to a fault, and an animal lover. There is an understanding within me that he will never be able to be the man I wished he was, but I can accept the man he is.

Now, saying that is one thing and living it is another. The only way I survive that relationship is with clear, loving boundaries.

I could easily stay stuck in the painful part of our relationship and use it to define me, keep me stuck in the story, that terrible groove full of lint and pain, and never come out. Being stuck in the hurt and devastation he caused while active in his addiction would be as easy as memory. But does it serve me? Do I wish I had an apology for every time he evoked amnesia about his behavior, absofuckinglutely.

But that will never happen. It's my choice to forgive him and not forget what he's capable of. That conscious choice makes it possible for us to have a relationship, and it helps inform how I choose to interact with him now.

So how does that equate to the pain you endured? Some wounds take years to heal and might be so colossal and unimaginable that others could never understand the depth. If you take the blame for any of that, that's what I suggest healing first, because you did nothing to deserve being treated like that, and there's nothing you could do that warrants being beaten or abused in any way.

I've read stories about people who forgive those who do unspeakable things to them. I admire their ability to say it and mean it. I believe those people are connected to God. Those who forgive horrific people are connected to the highest vibration of love and it supports them in letting go so their pain neither defines nor destroys them.

When a person doesn't forgive, it becomes an exchange of negative energy. In my experience, the person who did the hurting doesn't give much thought to what they did. But the person who has been hurt will spin out of control and cling to it.

Here's where I'll confess how I'm not always the highest-self version of myself. I'm the very human pissed off woman who doesn't forgive the person who did me wrong. I know it's not good for me, and I do what I can to get to a place of forgiving, but until that point in time, I do the best thing I know how. I treat myself kindly and I create boundaries.

Here's where I do the work on myself: the little girl who is triggered and crying, the woman whose abandonment wound is reopened, and I work to heal my shit. I can't make another person behave in the way I'd like. I can speak my truth, tell someone they hurt me, and then – here's the tricky bit – have no expectation for how they react to my truth.

That's the secret sauce. To be brave enough to tell a person they hurt you, without being vindictive or out for revenge, and then let it go. The magic happens when you give your thoughts and feelings a voice and have no expectation about the reaction.

HOLLY'S HEALING TIP
Forgiveness doesn't require two people to participate.
It only involves you.

If it's not safe or appropriate to speak to the person who hurt you, I highly suggest writing a letter. Get it out. Suck the poison from your body and soul. Trap the monster on paper. After you write the letter and are confident in what it says, burn it. Tear it into tiny pieces and free yourself. Kill the monster keeping you stuck and missing out. It's essential to burn things with love and light and make sure you're safe!

Then give yourself time to heal. Find family, friends, and professionals to help you heal. It always comes back to you. Forgive yourself because you ought to love the person with whom you'll spend the rest of your life. You did the best with what you knew, and now you know more.

HOLLY'S HEALING HOMEWORK:

Make a list of the ways in which you judge yourself harshly.

Write a forgiving sentence for each of the ways you listed above.
Read three of the above sentences aloud every day for the next thirty days.
I forgive myself for:

I forgive myself for:

I forgive myself for:

Write the name of the person you need to forgive. Feel free to do this on a separate sheet of paper if seeing the name is a trigger for you. Let the pain of the relationship and experience emerge from your body. Pull it out of your heart and gut, and then release the physical pain associated with it. Write down all of the words you wish you could say to them. Tear it up, burn it, or flush the letter down the toilet. Literally, free yourself from the past.

When you're done with that, write a letter to yourself, forgiving yourself for choosing to stay. Acknowledge you did your best with the tools you had and the place in which you found yourself. Forgive yourself for not knowing, doing, or being better. Tell yourself you love who you are. Tell yourself you're going to be okay, and things will get better. You deserve better. It wasn't your fault. You are loved and lovable. You matter.

GUIDED MEDITATION

Find a comfortable and nurturing place. It can be the sofa, someplace outside, snuggled in your bed, anywhere you feel the safest to be vulnerable. Settle into the space. Notice if you have tension in your neck or jaw, if you're sucking in your stomach, or if your shoulders are shrugged and tight. Consciously relax the muscles you are clenching. Take a deep breath in and sigh it out. Breathe into the places that are constricted in your body and exhale tightness.

Is your mind running away? Take note of where your thoughts go. Don't admonish yourself for how your mind works. It's okay. Meditation takes practice.

Some of you may benefit from playing a sound machine and having ocean waves or rain sounds playing while you relax. Others may want to try classical or binaural music. Anything that helps you relax is good.

Breathe in quiet, sigh, and say, "Aaaah."

Then, turn your attention to your heart. Is there a pain there that bubbles up? What do you call this pain? You may think of it as a manifestation of unkindness. It is the internal voice that hurts you. This is not what the heart chakra is supposed to be. The heart is meant for unconditional love.

It's time to love yourself unconditionally.

Forgive yourself for ever believing you were, or still are, less-than.

In the safe place you are in as you read this, invite healing angels to sit with you. Imagine their beautiful wings cocooning you. Their wings are soft and brush against your skin. The wings are soft pink and white. Your angels are giving you a mother's hug. It is how you have always wanted to be held. They don't let go, and in this space, they whisper, "It's okay. You're safe. I'm not going anywhere. Let it go. Let go of your fears and self-loathing. We forgive you."

Remember to breathe. With each breath in, receive the love and light the angels have for you. Say, "I forgive myself for being so hard on myself. I forgive myself for holding on to what no longer serves me. I let it go and am ready to receive healing."

Turn your hands so your palms face up. Sit in the stillness of receiving forgiveness and love for two minutes. If you want to stay in this peaceful place for longer, please do. Your angels are there for you. They are holding you and protecting you from negativity. They are giving you the tools you require to forgive yourself and to continue on your healing journey. Remember to love yourself through the changes.

This meditation helps you change your vibration to receive a higher frequency of love and light.

When you're ready, say one of your forgiving statements you wrote earlier out loud. Take note of how it feels to say it and hear it spoken aloud. Own this gift you give to yourself. Let the tears come. Let the smile appear across your face, or the feelings of peace settle into your body.

Take another deep breath in and let it out. Breathe in peace and exhale judgment. Breathe in love and exhale derision. For your last deep breath, breathe in self-love and exhale pain. Amen.

When you're ready, place your hands over your heart, sealing in the love and healing you received. Then open your eyes. You may want to write down the sensory details of this meditation in a journal. Or you may want to sit quietly for a few minutes more. Do what feels right for you. There is no need to rush.

I highly recommend taking a salt bath, with Epsom salts, tonight to aid in the healing process. There are many brands and scents to choose from, whether you prefer lavender for calming or a eucalyptus bath that helps to ease muscles and raise your vibration. But good old-fashioned Epsom salts work just fine, too. The salt bath will remove the negativity from your body and wash away the old. It's both symbolic and real, and it is a fantastic way to demonstrate self-care.

Please refrain from alcohol or any other self-numbing activities during this time of healing. Those self-soothing methodologies will undermine the high vibrational healing you are tackling. Numbing pain does not heal it. That is an old pattern you have outgrown. You have to name your pain and forgive yourself for any self-harm with a clear mind and spirit.

I know you can do it. I believe in you.

Eight

What is a boundary, and how do I get one?

Becoming the real you should feel awesome, but it will be hard to maintain this newfound self-love without a simple energetic tool. That tool is a boundary.

A boundary helps create a safe space near your heart and self. Think of it as an auric layer two to three feet around you, and everything on the inside of that is all you. It is your soul's dominion in this life. I have a simple meditation to share that I will teach you in a step-by-step way to set an energetic boundary.

A boundary is good. It equates with healthy self-respect and understanding your limits. It's a line you are unwilling to cross because to do so is detrimental to your well-being or another person's well-being.

You'll learn how to set a boundary in incremental steps.

Step one: How to say, "No"

This two-letter word is a major tool in your self-worth, self-care arsenal. It's time to shift the paradigm about the word "No" from a negative to a positive. When you master the concept of saying, "No," you carry a powerful tool in self-care. Because when you say "No" to others, you are saying "Yes" to you.

Did you know there are over seven thousand known languages on the planet? I bet when you read the words nein, non, lo, and niet, most of you understand they all mean "No." That is quite powerful.

You may not speak any language other than English, yet you understood "No" in other languages.

In English, the word "No" consists of two letters. Two little letters that can pack a punch when we hear them. Amazingly, something so small can have a significant effect on us.

Why is this? I'm convinced we misinterpret the word. We forget that the first time we heard the term "No," it was out of love. No was said to protect us and save us from pain.

"No, don't put your hand on the stove."

"No, don't shove crayons up your nose."

"No! Don't run with scissors."

Let's move on to our teenage years. Teens test boundaries with more force and will. As adults, we understand kids require structure and rules. It's easy to spot a teen without them, as they're out of control. No one is telling them no.

"No, you can't do what you want and fail out of school."

"No, you can't drive the car alone with just your permit."

"No, you can't get a tattoo."

"No, you can't go out until you finish your homework."

"No, you can't get in a car with a person I've never met."

"No, you can't spend twenty hours gaming."

In hindsight, we understand, though we still may not like that "No" was used as a way to keep us from making regrettable choices or mistakes. However, the "No" may have protected us from being at the wrong place at the wrong time, and maybe "No" helped some to finish school.

The problem lies in when people internalize that they were not smart enough to make their own decisions. They may have told themselves, "My parents don't trust me or my judgment. They don't understand me." Then the body absorbed that feeling.

When I was younger, I didn't understand my empathic and intuitive abilities and how they were my motivations to please people. I felt the energy coming at me, I knew when people were unhappy and hurting, and I was nice, so I wanted to help. I couldn't say "No" to anyone. I was willing to exhaust myself spiritually, emotionally, and physically to prevent anyone else from feeling hurt.

The height of this behavior manifested in my twenties. I could tick off all of those boxes of how a child of an alcoholic behaved. I sought approval. I was afraid of angry people, had abandonment issues, as well as an over-developed sense of responsibility and guilt at the thought of standing up for myself. I judged myself harshly and stuffed my feelings down with food and alcohol. I mimicked what I knew even when I hated what I was doing. It was my normal, and I didn't know how to escape the pathology.

Saying "No" to *anyone* was the last thing I'd do. I wanted to help people feel better. I was convinced I had the power to comfort everyone. I was afraid if I didn't support someone, they would leave me.

This fear of abandonment is what I call my emotional story.

HOLLY'S HEALING TIP
Giving is good, but giving yourself away is not.

We tell ourselves a caring person wouldn't hurt another person or deny anyone anything. It's as if "No" becomes the enemy. We forget how "No" is said out of love and protection. The shift I want to help create is how to use "No" is a tool of self-love and protection. I want to teach you what took me years to learn. Giving is good, but giving yourself away is not.

There came a time in my life when I understood my emotional story and system of beliefs wasn't working. I was exhausted. I had a short fuse and felt empty inside. I didn't want to be that person, so I worked hard to change. I learned to protect myself and took the time I needed to recharge and refuel my mind, body, and spirit. There are times when I regress, sure, but for the most part, I'm a self-care and boundary warrior now.

I see many clients come in and share their stories with me. A story can be a family pathology, emotional trauma, loss, or disappointment. Their belief system defines them and holds them back. The story justifies their behavior, and it reinforces limiting beliefs. The story is emotionally true, but holding on to it doesn't make room for healing or happiness. They are stuck in what they know, even when they realize what they know isn't working.

Other people and other people's needs become more important than taking care of themselves. They don't make room for self-care because part of their story is how "so and so needs me. I have to help them," or "This happened to me, so now this is how I act." They're sad and in pain. They're holding on to old thoughts and feelings that lock them in place.

To heal the past, we need to acknowledge the pain that feeds your fears. Then we have to heal it. An unhealed wound allows fear and pain to fuel how we react to people and situations. I believe that decisions made in fear probably aren't the best ones. Your fears even affect how you treat yourself.

Tell me, here and now, do you put yourself last?

It's an easy thing to get used to doing, what with life requiring so much juggling. It's sometimes easier to take care of other's needs first. Sometimes people even hide behind being busy because when you are busy, you don't have time to feel what's going on inside you.

My client's mother battled a terminal illness for two years. Her emotional truth in her family dynamic was that she was the strong one. She also happens to be the one without children and the one with a reliable job. During the many hospital visits her mother needed to make, the woman made multiple cross-country flights. She helped manage the doctors, the bills, and the medications, along with sitting by her mother's side. Her sisters let her. Even though her siblings lived in the same city as her sick mother, they expected her to fly in almost every weekend to handle things. And she did. She also gained thirty pounds and got depressed.

Do you know what she confessed to me? She said she wished she could just stay home because she was exhausted. She told me how heartbroken she was. She felt responsible for how everyone else was coping, and it was her job to make it easier. She told me about her pain. I held space for her and her pain. I supported her, and I energetically released the grip her guilt had. We worked on getting to the place where she could forgive herself for putting her needs last. Her guides supported her in her grief, and she learned how to say, "No."

Caring for a parent brings out all sorts of family dynamics and patterns. Caretakers become exhausted and often don't have time to cope with their feelings, and instead turn on other family members for playing the parts and roles they did as children.

But you need to sit and feel your feelings. Instead of doing it all, say, "I can't," or "I need help," or maybe even a clear "No."

"No" because my heart is breaking, and this is too much for me. Or, "I can't afford to fly back and forth." Or, "No, I have to take care of myself and not lose my job."

If you take care of your family like that, I bet you take care of some of your friends emotionally, physically, and spiritually, too.

It's what you know.

I used to have lots of energy vampire friends, the kind of people who took and stole my energy. If you don't like the term vampire, then think mosquito. They suck the blood from you, too. They were people who wanted things from me, whether it was free readings, a favor, a ride, or help watching their kids while they went out. Once upon a time, I gave into them, but not anymore.

I learned how to love and protect myself. I know when I need time alone to process and decompress. Sometimes I need time to pout and react. I believe we have to feel our feelings. Move through them, and then get over them. When we push things down or inside because someone else may need us more, we aren't honoring ourselves. We're hiding in being busy. We magically think, *If I ignore it, it will go away.* Or, *If I'm helpful, things will get better.*

What needs to happen is you need to speak up for yourself. Practice self-love and protection. You need to put yourself first so you can be whole and embodied. Then, when you show up to help another person, you model something magnificent. There are real tangible fears that get stirred up when making changes in life, fears about saying, "No." By facing them together, I hope to ease you into them and change them from big, looming monsters to dust bunnies.

Do you own your fears?

As I mentioned earlier, my favorite definition of fear is:

FALSE EVIDENCE APPEARING REAL

There are a couple of others that float around: Forget Everything And Run and Face Everything And Rise. Healing is an evolution. This is one of those times when it is important to dig deeper into your fear and heal at another level.

The truth is your fear about how someone will respond to what you have to say or do is probably far worse than the reality of the situation. If you're anything like I used to be, your mind can spin and make up ridiculous stories that stress you out. Your fear stops you from creating a healthy boundary, recognizing your truth, and your ability to say no.

An example of this is how one time someone at work bought me a fancy coffee. It was a lovely gesture, except I didn't like the coffee. I can't remember what kind it was, but let's say it was a macchiato. I prefer coffee strong with cream and sugar. So here I am with an expensive cup of coffee, and I didn't want it or like it. I became paralyzed by my fear of hurting their feelings if I didn't accept it and drink it. Since I acted like I wanted it, the person continued to bring me this type of coffee.

I spent *nine months* thinking about all the kind ways I could tell the person, "I don't want this coffee. Please stop bringing it to me." I practiced what to say during my commute. I sweat, thinking about how mean and selfish I was, until one day, I finally just told the person, "Hey, you know what? I just like my coffee plain with cream and sugar." My hands and armpits were sweaty. My heart pounded in my chest. I may have had a dramatic roll of sweat coming from my brow. I was so afraid of what would happen next.

You know what happened? He said, "Okay."

It didn't matter. See what I mean about fear? My fear of hurting the other person was all make-believe. It wasn't real because what I said didn't hurt. Fear had me conjure all sorts of emotional demons and triggers. It played out hundreds of scenarios in which I was a terrible person, and anxiety told me to hold my tongue. Fear is a deceiver. It's time to shut it up.

Let's call out the top fears about saying "No," so they can't make you spin and waste your time and energy. Remember, we're going to consciously transform the word "no" into an act of self-love and self-care. Read that sentence again, this time with your hands over your heart. I want you to take that in.

HOLLY'S HEALING TIP
Consciously transform the word "no"
into an act of self-love and self-care.

I want to remind your soul that "no" is meant to protect you from harm and over-giving, and is a loving boundary.

Six Common Fears to Transform:

1: If I say "No," I'll hurt their feelings.

Like my coffee situation, are you worried about something that may not actually be true?

Saying "no" may disappoint someone, but most people know when they ask for something, there's a fifty-fifty chance the answer will be yes or no. Saying no does not mean you wish the person asking ill will or pain. It just means you aren't able to do whatever it is that is being asked of you. So really, it won't hurt their feelings. This is a boundary that acknowledges your limits.

2: If I say "No," they won't like me.

I'll still be your friend if you say no. I'll respect the fact that you know yourself and are able to acknowledge how you aren't able to help.

If you lose a friend because you said no to something they asked, I'm going to say it doesn't feel like a good friendship. Would a person who respects and cares for you discard you so easily?

A friendship should be mutual, with give and take. Of course, there are highs and lows to every relationship. But fear should not be part of it.

I like using the analogy of make-believe children. If your child came home and said, "Fran said she won't be friends with me anymore because I didn't let her cheat off my paper," I'm guessing your response would be something like, "Fran sucks, and you don't need her."

If your child said, "Fran wanted my lunch money, but I said no, and now Fran isn't talking to me," again, you might say, "Good riddance."

So why is it harder to say "no" as a grown-up? It shouldn't be.

A consequence of saying "Yes" all the time is you may be asked for more and more significant favors. Once you start saying "Yes," saying "No," gets harder. The person asking may be able to twist your words and feelings to manipulate and guilt you. Those people are vampires. When you say no to this kind of person, you set a boundary for not being used.

3: If I say "No" at work, who will do the job?

There are times in life when you find yourself carrying another person's load. But I'm guessing your body will give you clues and cues when you're doing too much. When I worked at Spelling Television, I did most of my boss's job because he was "training" me. All the while, though, you know what I figured out? He wasn't training me. He was just getting paid three times as much as me for doing less. It wasn't until I summoned my courage and said, "No," then raised my voice and made some noise about my job, that things changed. Because the truth is, *we teach people how to treat us.* I showed my bosses I could be used and underpaid. Then I had to go and change that. In doing so, I created a boundary of self-respect.

4: If I say "No," my friends will forget me.

This is the fear of being left out. This one once plagued me. I sincerely believed I was forgettable, and if I wasn't doing everything my friends did, I'd be forgotten.

With Facebook and Instagram, this one can sting. We've all been the person not in the photos, and it sucks. It's in those "poor me" moments that we forget Facebook and Instagram aren't real. They're curated images filtered to perfection. Pictures aren't relationships. Your friends shouldn't forget about your friendship just because you say "No" to helping them or going out together. Real friendships are based on mutual respect and affection. The real you knows what you can afford and when you require and deserve rest. This boundary respects your energy.

5: If I say "No," and it's the weekend, I feel like there's no way to refuse.

You deserve time off, too. Weekends can be more hectic with carpooling kids to activities, shopping, laundry, cleaning, mowing the lawn, and paying bills. So, if you have a free hour, why not enjoy it? Their needs are not more important than yours. You matter. Your health and well-being count. This is another example of a boundary that is created to make room for what you want and need.

6: If I say "No" to my kids, I fill with guilt.

Kids are resilient, and they will deal if you don't participate and celebrate everything they do. Please don't raise narcissists. Don't teach children that they are the center of the universe, or that their every whim should be granted. Teach them how to cope with frustration and adversity, two essential life skills.

Here's an example for parents with elementary, school-aged children. Set expectations at the beginning of the year. Explain to them how you'll be a room parent, or help out in the classroom twice this year and offer the things and the time you're willing and able to give. If you don't fill in your name on all of the sign-up sheets, it gives someone else the chance to sign up.

Then, don't beat yourself up for saying, "No." Instead, remind yourself you're teaching your children that, as adults, they will have multiple priorities. You're modeling how they can make choices when they grow up. Sometimes kids' desires aren't the most important, and learning to cope with disappointment is a valuable skill to have.

Learning to say "No," and practicing it clearly, demonstrates how you value yourself and your time. You are teaching people, including your children, how to treat you by how you treat yourself.

Saying "No" is a demonstration of self-love. You are protecting yourself from anything harmful or damaging to your mind, body, and spirit. That harmful thing includes over-scheduling and over-promising.

I hope by acknowledging these fears, you regain the power they have been holding over you.

How does people-pleasing make you feel?

Another side effect of not saying "No" is resentment. Do you keep tabs or a list of what you've done for a friend or family member? Do you start feeling like things aren't fair? Do you ever look around at the people you love and help, and think, *Why don't you ever help me?* Maybe you're a person who never asks for help. When I was busy being a people pleaser, I never asked for help. I was stoic and determined to do it on my own. But guess what? We all need help every now and again. Asking for what you need does not diminish the result when you receive it. People actually like knowing what you want and need.

There's another dangerous consequence to saying "Yes" all the time. Do you say "Yes" to doing a favor or taking on more work when you don't have the time to do it? Regardless of your capacity to do the task, and despite your best intentions, you might not do the favor on time, or you miss the deadline, and then the person you said you'd help might get mad at you. That's a lot to juggle, and additionally, by saying "Yes" to helping out, you're self-sabotaging. You possibly already know you can't get it done, and you know the person asking for help is going to end up being upset, yet you don't stop yourself because of which fear?

The situation is like a snake eating its tail in a never-ending cycle. Your fear of not being liked gets triggered, and you feel guilty and start the entire process over again. It's time to stop doing that. Find your voice and use the word "no" as self-love and protection from harm.

There's a hidden agenda for a people-pleaser too. Being super busy is a coping mechanism. If you're busy helping others, you don't have time to cope with what's going on for you. But I promise you can process and get through the very things you're avoiding and feel better after.

The goal is to be real, not perfect. I'm asking you to be aware of what's not working for you. I want you to be mindful of the feelings you're carrying inside of your body and address them. Feeling something won't kill you. It can be downright unpleasant, but I promise that you will feel so much better when you work through the feelings and release that energy. You will no longer be ruled by fear.

Is a boundary rigid?

A boundary isn't a wall or a massive defense mechanism. It doesn't mean you're prepped and ready for a fight. It isn't a mask you wear, so people won't know or recognize you. A boundary is an energetic line that you don't allow others to cross. It helps create a safe space. That space can be a few feet around you and it can also be as big as your home.

HOLLY'S HEALING TIP
A boundary is an energetic line that you don't let others cross.

HOLLY'S HEALING HOMEWORK:

Practice saying "no." Repeat the word without any context and see if merely saying it conjures any unease. Once you get the hang of saying the word aloud, try using it.

Ask a friend to help you practice saying no by acting as the person to whom you're afraid to say it. Ask the friend to role-play being difficult so you can face all of your fears without any consequences.

Write all of the things this exercise made you feel.

Write what you hoped to feel instead.

If saying "no" is still a challenge, see the following tips to help you master the skill. Remember that learning a new skill takes practice, patience, and persistence.

Ten Ways To Say "No":
1. Remember, "no" is said out of self-love and protection.
2. Don't answer someone's request right away. Give yourself time to evaluate the situation. Breathe in for a count of 4 and breathe out for a count of 8. Do that three times.
3. Evaluate their needs, along with your own. Do they need help specifically from you, or are they calling because they know you always say yes? Do you want to help? Do you have other things planned at the time they are requesting?
4. Just because you feel another person's pain doesn't mean you have to heal it. This is especially true for people with empathetic abilities.
5. Ask yourself what will happen if you say "No"? Will the person come to serious harm?
6. If you can't say "No" on the phone, text it. "Sorry, I can't." Keep it short. No story.
7. Be polite and firm. Believe it yourself.
8. Don't go on and on. A person wanting your help may be able to talk you out of your own story.
9. Be honest with yourself.
10. Protect your downtime. You deserve to relax, recharge, and rest. You don't have to give in to others to the point of exhaustion.

It's hard to stop doing what you know. It takes patience and a process to shift what you've always done and adopt a new way of being. It takes courage to do this. You may be a bit aggressive at first or weak in establishing your boundaries, but it's okay. It will get easier and become second nature soon enough.

GUIDED MEDITATION

Saying "No" and enforcing a boundary may stir anxiety. That's normal. This is a new skill, and being nervous about new things is common. This meditation will support your desire to create a safe space around you, along with healthy boundaries.

Take a moment to settle into wherever you're located. Close your eyes, get comfortable, and feel how much space you occupy. I want you to notice your breath, but not change how you breathe.

Now, breathe in and acknowledge how your body feels. Are you uncomfortable, tired? Are you carrying a weight that isn't yours? Are you aware of the mass of your physical body as it rests on a chair?

Breathe out and let tension go. Then, breathe in and fill up with universal love before breathing out stress. Breathe in peace and breathe out judgment. I want you to visualize yourself outside in a sun-flecked clearing in the woods. There is a comfortable place for you to rest in this clearing. It can be the ground, a blanket, or even a hammock. There is no wrong way to be here.

Settle into your comfortable spot. Breathe in the fresh air, the smell of pine, and clean air. In this peaceful place, you are able to connect with guides, angels, and unconditional love. Breathe in acceptance and exhale conditions. From this place of love and safety, create an energetic boundary. Repeat after me:

I honor the spirit inside me.

I honor the loving spirits around me, both seen and unseen.

I release any energy that is not mine and return it to the person to whom it belongs. If they can't handle it, I ask that it be held in a safe space until they can.

151

Imagine wide paths leading to your place in the woods. Visualize the people whose energy you are holding onto as though they too are standing on those trails. These are the people you feel responsible for helping. They are those to whom you have the hardest time saying, "No.".

Once you can see these people in your mind's eye, turn them into a faded image, like a filter you use in an app. Dim them. Mute their intensity. Then, imagine this person walking away from you. Envision them carrying bags, rocks, or sizzling with the energy you carried for them. Watch as they walk away. Do this without the need for revenge or to cause them any pain. Let it all go with love and light.

After you witness the energy walking away, you can imagine the trail fading away, too. It is no longer attached to your safe place. See a bright white light filling the space where the roads once were. The light is a filter; it won't allow for negativity. Instead, it heals the ground and flowers, and ferns begin to bloom where the trail once was. Take a deep breath in, sigh it out, and enjoy the release of tension.

Call back any energy that you may have given away and ask that if be cleansed in God's heavenly light and returned to you.

I'd like you to imagine a beautiful mix of ultraviolet, pink, and lavender rain coming down on you. It's all of the energy you gave away. All of those pieces of you that you may have neglected or lost while you were so busy doing for others. Let the beautiful, multicolored rain warm your body. Allow it to sink into your skin and fill you up. Allow your singular energy, the very light of your soul, to reconnect and nourish your body. Let it bring peace and serenity to you. Allow yourself to release any pent-up energy.

You may find yourself crying or notice a change in your breathing. It's okay. Continue to receive the unconditional love the universe wants to return to you. Let it fill all of the spaces you once used to hold onto other people's stuff. Your body should feel lighter.

At this point, honor God. Visualize God as a golden light blooming full of love all around you. Breathe in this image. Breathe out. Get comfortable. Know that it is love and light, and it's meant to protect you. Then, say, "Amen."

And there you have it. You set a boundary, let go of what no longer serves you, and took care of yourself. You did it with the intention to protect yourself. You created the boundary from love.

Nine

How do I take care of myself?

Now that you have a boundary, here's a way to look at it. Boundaries are self-care. Inside the boundary, you have the space to feel your feelings. You won't be distracted by the drama and noise you don't want in your life.

A boundary gives you space to heal. Once you heal those systems and ways of being that you know aren't working for you, you can create new ones that work for you. You become the person you want to be, the real you. You can be your authentic, happy self.

What do I mean when I tell you to feel your feelings?

At this point in your healing journey, it's time to take everything to a deeper level. When I talk about feeling your feelings, I mean you can't run away from that pain inside of you.

Please don't judge the source of your wound. The incident that created it doesn't have to be as traumatic as something like losing your home or death. Any moment in your life that irrevocably changed how you see the world and interact in it matters. This includes feeling ignored, belittled, and used in relationships. Another way to process this is to think about the people who left fingerprints and scars on your self-worth and heart.

Until now, your reaction to that event was your normal. But you came to a point where what you knew no longer worked for you. The definition you had for yourself was as uncomfortable as a pair of too-tight jeans. No one likes being squeezed into a mold not meant for them.

The emotion I ran away from until I was thirty was anger. I was subconsciously afraid of it because that feeling belonged to my father. I didn't understand I fueled my ambitions with anger. When people told me, "You can't," the voice inside of my head said, *fuck you, I'll show you! I'll prove I can.* The anger fueled me until it ran out. Like fossil fuel, it dried up, and I was left empty and unable to move.

HOLLY'S HEALING TIP
Anger is motivation's fossil fuel.
It's dirty, finite, and bad for the environment.

Many successful people share this fire-fueled motivation. However, I dare say not many are happy or healthy. It took the world I built ending for me to own my part in its demise.

I had to *feel* the hurt behind the anger to heal. I had to look inward at myself and decipher what I was made of and what I lost along the way. If you deny experiencing an emotion vehemently, then I'm going to take an educated guess that your guides are laughing at you, and it's exactly that feeling which you must explore.

You must identify the emotion you're using to define yourself, figure out why you feel it, then heal that wound and get on with life. That's what I mean when I say you have to feel it to heal it. It means sink into the heart of yourself and be honest with what's going on there.

There are no good or bad feelings. There's no room for judgment in this phase. There should only be unconditional love and forgiveness. When you identify those feelings that control you, they lose power over you. These emotional breakthroughs are a miraculous release. The weight of the pain you've been living with will be gone, making room in your body and soul for the new you. You'll access your intuition and recognize, sort, and create a boundary between you and drama. You'll receive energy from a loving source instead of a dead one.

What is self-care?

Once you get the hang of saying "no," what will you do with the oodles of free time you managed to claim? Who says you have to always be doing? What if you could enjoy downtime? Read a book. Take a bath and let your mind wander. Take time to remember the magnificent being you are. Free yourself of relationships that diminish you, and find ones that uplift.

Self-care reconnects you to your thoughts, feelings, and desires. Your mind, heart, and gut should be in alignment. If there is a disconnect, it's a cue that there is more healing work to be done.

There are many ways to take care of yourself, including eating right, exercising, having no debt, and treating yourself to clothes you love. Many women enjoy manicures and pedicures, getting their hair done by professionals, traveling, and having healthy relationships. Men enjoy a round of golf or watching a favorite sport. All of those are important for a happy life, but I want to take you one step further.

157

Self-care feeds your soul. It's a happiness that doesn't depend on your dress size or the amount of money in your wallet. Self-care is vital for every person on the planet. It revitalizes the spirit and energizes the body. It's joyous and fun and not about being selfish.

The pandemic has heightened our need for self-care. Fear, illness, and quarantine have impacted everyone's mental, emotional, and spiritual well-being. In the past, I used to recommend being in the physical presence of friends and family to hug and laugh with them in person. In today's world, this isn't possible. Connection while remaining safe may require a screen, and screens aren't warm or loving.

It's time to think outside of the box. We must appreciate the small pleasures in life — the moments you can have. For me, self-care includes going outside and connecting with nature. Self-care is a salt bath, painting my own nails, and watching make-up tutorials. I feel better when I can sit and read near my husband, and when I listen to my child talk about her day.

Self-care doesn't happen online. Posting images and waiting for approval isn't what I'm asking you to do. I want you to dig deeper and honor the smallest things that make you feel good.

I'll give you an example of what self-care was for me pre-pandemic. I have always loved dancing. On Thursday nights, I used to drive forty-five minutes to take an African dance class. Nothing made me feel joy like I felt when I was there.

The class was challenging and fun. I found community with the people. I'm pretty sure I had a smile on my face the entire time I was dancing, and the whole drive home.

I lose time when I dance. I don't check my phone. There is nothing else but drums, rhythm, and dance. When I'm in class, I'm not responsible for anything and there's no expectations on me.

I get that way when I walk in nature, whether on a beach or in the mountains. I reach my spirit out and connect energetically with the landscape. I feel the same way when I dig in the dirt to garden and when I have a good book in my hands. People often refer to Mother Nature as Gaia. The goddess Gaia is the embodiment of Mother Earth and her grounding, healing, creative, and nurturing power.

Quarantined self-care may include cooking or baking. It can be picking up a pencil and trying to draw. You may fingerpaint with your family or learn how to crochet or sew. This is a time to discover your love for gardening or running. All of these things are possible during quarantine, and you can continue them long after.

If these options overwhelm you, spend five minutes doing whatever it is that makes you happy. No matter how busy you are, you can take five minutes for yourself. Maybe sit outside with your face in the sun and be still enough to hear the leaves rustle.

If this is not part of your life, it may sound challenging. But I know you can do it because I was able to make those changes.

At my people-pleasing worst, I did nothing to nurture myself. I was in an emotionally and verbally abusive relationship. I was convinced that if I loved the man enough, I could make him happy. I stopped doing everything I loved as a means of pleasing him. This is utter bullshit. You can't make another person happy.

159

You can only do that for yourself. Happiness comes from inside.

HOLLY'S HEALING TIP
Happiness comes from within.

It took me imagining having children in this relationship and asking myself if my situation was good enough for them. I questioned myself, "Is this what you want to teach your children? Is this love good enough for them?" When the answer was, "Hell, no!" I had to find the courage — despite my brokenness and fear, and say, "No!" to him, to the relationship, and to my willingness to put myself last.

When we agreed to separate, I rented a convertible car, played music loud in the house, danced, wrote, and went out with friends. I did all of the things I had stopped doing so I could make him happy, and, in doing so, I began to remember who I was and what recharged my soul. When I took off my wedding ring, I felt unshackled and free from a commitment to being viewed as less-than.

I remember a phone conversation with my brother during this time. He said, "You know, the things you want in a partner aren't uncommon. They're pretty basic."

Back then, I think my must-have list included: Will go out. Doesn't fall asleep at 9 PM. Talks to me. Looks at me kindly. Wants to touch me.

Soon after we separated, a co-worker stopped in my office and said, "It's nice to see you smile. You haven't smiled in a long time."

That struck me. I have always been known for my big smile. How had I lost so much of myself? The loss was made possible by my lack of boundaries, as well as my fears, lack of self-esteem, and inability to stand up for what I needed and deserved. It was rooted in the belief that I had to make sacrifices for love in order to receive it. I vowed to change all of that.

It can be difficult to remember how you're responsible for your own happiness. It may seem impossible, but I promise you it's true and worth the effort.

HOLLY'S HEALING TIP
You don't have to sacrifice to love in order to receive it.

Saying "No," Part Two:

When you say "No" to the things that put you last or don't really matter, you have time to remember or discover what does. And you know what does matter? You. You matter. When you get the hang of saying "No," you create space to love yourself. You can care for the parts of yourself that are worn out and let them rejuvenate.

Do you trust that you know what's best for you? Knowing something and doing it are very different. Accepting that you're hanging in there emotionally, physically, or spiritually, but giving whatever energy you have to another, isn't doing anyone any good. If you're not okay, how can you be any help to anyone else?

Your guides want you to take off the cement-filled backpack of co-dependence. It's heavy and making your neck hurt. You don't need a relationship to define your worth. You can make choices without assuaging the needs of a partner. This is self-care. Making time for yourself to sort out what you want, and then doing it.

What is the other trope we hear? It is how a butterfly must break free of its cocoon. It must stretch and dry its wings to fly. Maybe you and the person you're entwined with both need time to strengthen your wings. Perhaps the other person needs to stand on his own, and you need to do the same. People seem to forget they can survive growing pains. It seems we're wired as a species to not learn too much while we're happy. There is no growth when we're comfortable.

Life will hand you lemons and thorns. How you react to them shapes your life. Learning when you need self-care is a powerful lesson. When you get good at taking the time you need, you'll be a happier person. Your emotional, spiritual, and mental tank will be full. You won't run on empty.

Working through feelings is hard. I reach out to my guides and pray to receive the help I need. They're always there. I talk a lot when I'm emotional. I get loud. I cry. I go inside and sometimes push everyone away. I have to sort through all of the issues I have, and when I work through it all, I come out on the other side whole. I make new choices.

There will be times in life when there are emergencies and stress, but there are also times when it's okay to utilize your boundaries, speak your truth, and take time to care for your mind, body, and soul. Take a salt bath and moisturize. Look up and see the real you. Love that person. Heal your hurt, and get on with living.

How do I stop myself from comparing myself to other people on social media?

Suppose I post a cute picture of the kitten we adopted and include the story of how my other cat was run over. We found him six miles away on the other side of a lake. We realized he had been taken, and he had tried running away from the person who took him before being killed by a car. My husband found him splayed on the side of the road after a stranger responded to my neighborhood post about our missing Ninja. I might add how our other cat yowled at night for weeks due to missing his brother, and how we decided to rescue another cat from the animal control shelter.

Is there a need in that story? A need to be seen as a good person because we rescue pets instead of buying from a breeder? Is there shame in our story because our cat got out and away? Is there public guilt because someone took him and he ended up so far away? Is there pride in knowing we saved another life when we weren't able to save his?

The answer is yes. But sharing all of these intimate details, along with filtered images, has become the norm. It's how we connect, process, gain acceptance, and earn a living.

I teach my child that people aren't who they represent on social media. Social media profiles are one piece of a carefully crafted image. Don't believe everything you see. You don't know what's going on in a person's life when the camera is off.

Self-care includes privacy. You don't have to sell an image. Remember how at the beginning of this book, we uncovered the real you? Not the you society says you have to be, not the you your family may require, but the you who is inside and yearning to come out?

I highly recommend not sharing this newly discovered vulnerable person on social media. Keep her close. Keep him safe. Give yourself the time to be comfortable in your own skin and learn to set boundaries, to say no, and to honor yourself when your soul needs recharging.

A screen will not make you feel better, just as likes from strangers don't define you. This transition is about holding true to who you are. You are precious. You are a gift.

HOLLY'S HEALING TIP
The world won't disappear if you don't post for a day or two.
Allow yourself to take time for self-care, and relish how magnificent it makes you feel.

Self-care is about checking in with how you're feeling emotionally, spiritually, and physically. People get so good at ignoring the signals their minds, bodies, and spirit provide. You may need to slow down and ask yourself:

Do you feel off?

Do you feel physical pain? If so, how long have you been ignoring it?

Does something about your situation feel wrong, but you can't name it?

Do you get an uneasy feeling around certain people? Do you ignore it? How much time do you spend with them?

Are you happy with your situation at work? In relationships? In health?

What does self-care have to do with any of these things?

Self-care means taking care of all of the above questions, and adding a dash of joy into your life as well. Self-care means addressing what isn't working and devoting yourself to finding a solution to what ails you. Transitions in life or feeling stuck are what bring people into my office to work with me. They want guidance and support moving forward. When I tap into your highest self and communicate with your guides, they share the messages they're trying to send you. Most times, people don't listen to messages. Messages may include illness, bad dreams, anxiety, feathers, noticeable shapes, birds, or even feeling a tingle on the back of your neck.

What are the signs you're missing?

Well, I asked you a series of questions above for a reason.

HOLLY'S HEALING TIP
You matter, and your happiness counts.

How you feel, from your aches and pains, to the things you suddenly notice, are all signs for you. I'm sure you acknowledge when your shoulders are tight, you're tense, and something is stressing you out. But what about the feathers you find when you're walking around?

Feathers mean you're on the right path, and you're receiving a gift to tell you so. Birds, on the other hand, represent so many things. They can be a spirit animal calling out to you to rejoice. Some birds are loved ones sending messages, and others still are your guides sending support. I have noticed that people often associate specific birds with family members. Most of the time, they come in the form of hummingbirds, cardinals, and hawks, because these types of birds evoke memories of the person who is missed.

You may notice you look at the clock at a specific time every day. Common spiritual messages come at 11:11. The popular belief around this time is that it's a message from an angel. I interpret it as a wink from high vibration energy aligning you to your highest self.

In general, seeing repeating numbers is translated to mean an angel of some kind is looking out for you. When I notice angelic numbers, I connect with my heart and say, "Thank you" to whoever and whatever is giving me a wink. I may meditate for a few moments to see if I can connect with my own message. I pay attention to what's happening to me, physically, mentally, and emotionally.

This does not mean that every random occurrence is a sign from God. I once saw a hysterically funny video about women talking about signs from God. If I remember correctly, one woman was stopped in traffic in front of a donut shop and knew it must be a sign to eat a donut. Another saw a shirt that said, "Fuck It" and said it was a sign to have an affair with her boss. These are meant to be funny. You can do the healing work and still maintain a sense of humor.

When you get in the habit of self-care, you won't want to lose it for any length of time. Why should you? If you take care of yourself, you aren't emotionally, mentally, or physically tired. You will attract new people and experiences into your life and have the ability to enjoy them. You are a precious gift. Treat yourself as such.

I recently had a client come to me and say, "I want to vibrate at a higher level. What measurable and quantifiable steps are there to do this?"

This client has deep-rooted family trauma and resentment. She wants to tell others how to be more intuitive and use herself as an example.

I smiled, and said, "You're asking for a to-do list."

She and I started to laugh, and I continued, "The first step for you is going to be to surrender."

"To what?" She didn't even let me finish my thought.

"Control."

"Oh," she flushed.

"And you're going to actually have to feel the feelings you're out here in the world trying to manage while you control everything around you."

"Yeah, I do that."

"And you're going to have to start loving your children unconditionally. Because the way you're doing it now teaches them that they have to be perfect for you to love them, and that's not a high vibration at all.

"You're right," she said. "I can do that."

"I know," I said, but my voice was soft and full of empathy because I knew this was part of her lesson. She wanted to do and be better.

The easiest way I can explain shifting or growing into new frequencies and higher vibrations is this: Imagine a time when the little things will stop bothering you. Think about unconditional love. Most people will use Jesus and Buddha as examples of high vibration souls. My interpretation is that those of us who are sensitive and can connect to the energy unseen have the ability to evolve and connect to higher and higher beings of light.

Beings of light are kind and loving. They do not judge our humanity or the mistakes we make. To them, it's part of the journey to evolve and grow. Just as we physically evolve from infant to adult, we can grow spiritually. That spiritual growth is connecting us to a higher vibration.

A significant portion of that client's self-care is to feel. Feel all the things she avoids. Heal her past and create a better future. It's one hundred percent possible, but it takes time, and it will require help along the way, including emotional honesty and vulnerability. There is no healing when you think it entails ticking items off off a to-do list. It requires diving deep into the well of your soul to free yourself from past, repressed hurts and pains. It means forgiving yourself and others.

Self-care means giving yourself permission and time to explore anything and everything in life that fills you with joy.

HOLLY'S HEALING HOMEWORK:

Remember, healing is a process. Be attentive to your undiscovered self. These self-care options are significant first steps. They may seem easy, but I promise they are vital and essential.

When was the last time you took care of yourself?

What did that look like?

Do you do what others like to do just to make things easy?

Remember, self-care is about what reinvigorates you. You don't need a partner to do this. Your own company is enough!

Do you surround yourself with people because they have the intelligence, faith, abilities, talent, flexibility, courage, or daring you wish you had? Think about them in a new way. Instead of wishing you had what they possess, think of each friend as a reflection of what is inside of you. Now is the perfect time to unlock the door and let that inclination/ voice/ dream/ desire out.

169

REAL, NOT PERFECT

Write down every time you stop yourself from doing anything because you put your family and others first. Make a different choice the next time.

Try doing something fun. An activity that has nothing to do with family obligations, kids' sports, extended family, or fixing anything. Go ice skating. Take a cooking class. Run as fast as you can to the corner and back. Blow bubbles. Play a favorite song really loud and dance around to it.

Write yourself a love letter. Permit yourself to sleep in one weekend day. Write down any signs you see, and then ask yourself what they mean. Sit quietly, and try getting still enough to see what thoughts and feelings come up. Write them all down.

What self-care action do you most identify with?

What self-care idea excites you the most?

Does the idea of self-care fill you with anxiety? If so, the first thing you need to begin healing is your self-worth.

When you transition from believing self-care is selfish to knowing that self-care heals you, makes you happy, makes you smile, gives you energy, and is safe and smart, you will then have successfully integrated it into your life.

GUIDED MEDITATION

I want you to get a piece of paper and something to write with, and then find a place that is peaceful and quiet. It can be someplace, whether inside or out, where you can be left alone for five minutes. You can be standing, sitting, or lying down. I want you to be at your most comfortable.

Take a deep breath in, and ground yourself as a means of creating a safe boundary for you to begin the self-care work. Feel the air around you and determine if it's still or moving. Pay attention to the senses that are filling your mind and what they entail. Don't fight the feelings or sensations; instead, observe them as you take deep breaths in and out. Try to slow down your breathing. Breathe in for the count of four: 1, 2, 3, 4. And out at the same pace: 1, 2, 3, 4.

Next, follow the same steps to the count of five.

Then, to the count of six.

Imagine yourself inside of a circle of healing where those loving guides, spirits, loved ones, and God surround you in peace and unconditional love. Nothing bad can come in; you are one hundred percent safe.

Inside this circle, relax into your body. Feel your soul in your skin. Notice your body's movements, but don't judge them. Think about loving yourself completely, including every inch, blemish, and perceived imperfection, as well as all of your talents and desires. I want you to be in this space and breathe them in. Take additional breaths in and out to the count of five: 1, 2, 3, 4, 5.

At this point, go past the physical manifestations of your soul and imagine a beautiful, bright white light, coming from the center of the Earth, from the Earth's star heart. That light comes up and around you in the circle, amplifying the protection around you as it grounds you in safety.

Feel the warmth and the texture of the light. Know this light is harmony, acceptance, and love.

You may experience emotional responses to this unconditional love and safety. That's good. It means you are receiving what you need and desire.

Stay in this safe place for a moment. Don't worry. Remember, you're perfectly safe, and you're not alone.

Without judging where your mind went during the silence, consider what feelings came up for you in the loving, healing space?

Did you sink into a place of deep comfort and trust, or were you triggered?

Ask yourself, what do I need most to care for myself right now? Write it down.

If your mind and judgment are getting in the way, write the question with your dominant hand, and when you go to answer, use your other hand. Using the other hand is a way to free your mind and loosen the need to control. It is also a technique used to teach people how to connect with their highest self.

If you've come to this meditation with a specific question in mind, do the same thing. Write the question down with your dominant hand and answer with the other.

Put the pen and paper down now.

Close your eyes and imagine yourself back in the middle of the healing circle. Palms are facing up. See yourself receiving all of the love surrounding you. Envision it as bright green poppies swirling around you like magic. See the green petals transform into light, and allow the light to sink into your body, energizing your cells and filling your heart with the most divine and fulfilling love. You deserve it. You're worth loving. The pain and wounds you have carried no longer serve you, and they are being healed by this light. You may experience a physical and emotional reaction to receiving this love. This is part of healing and raising your vibration.

It's an important step in self-care. This space helps you see with a clear vision and less ego what you need to work on. You don't have to heal it on your own. It's okay to ask for help. Help is waiting to be asked to assist you.

Wiggle your fingers and imagine the green attaching to your hands. The green may appear as gloves, rings, or orbs in the palms of your hands. Place your left hand over your heart and your right hand on top of your left.

Repeat after me:
I am worthy.
I am loved.
I am lovable.
Self-care starts with me.

As you practice meditation, consider some questions: Is there something you feel that you want healed? Is there an unnamed fear or wound holding you back? This is the place to heal it. Here, inside of the healing circle, created by you and supported by your guides, master light workers, and the unconditional loving spirit of God, you can let them go. Simply release the notion that you can't. Make a wish and let the universe help you to manifest it. Set a new intention to no longer focus on the wrong, and begin to pay attention to your happiness, your worthiness, your ability to be loved.

You are worth the time it takes to own your self-worth. You don't have to hold onto other people's limiting beliefs anymore. You are not the worst day of your life or the worst thing that happened to you. You are an infinite soul, who came into being to live and love. Honor your mind, body, and spirit. Honor the gift you are to this world. Be a representation of your highest self. This doesn't require you to be anything other than you. You don't have to be perfect. You can be honest with your thoughts and feelings. You can create and maintain boundaries and manifest a happy life.

Sit in this place of gratitude for as long as you're comfortable. If you feel like running from a vulnerable position, try to take three breaths before you leave.

To signal to the beings supporting you in the circle, it's time to enter this world again, place your palms flat to the earth, and thank them for their support and love. Wiggle your fingers and toes, and when you're ready, open your eyes and say, "Amen."

Take a moment to appreciate the work you did and the love you received. This is a good time to journal and record any thoughts, feelings, and sensations that the meditation may have created for you. Be sure to fully ground in the present before rushing back to your daily life.

Ten

What happens next?

I hope when you come upon this page, you've gained perspective about who you are and the relationships in your life.

I want you to own who you are and understand that you are lovable and deserve love from the very center of your being.

Let this newfound definition of self, of who you are inside and out, color your world with new appreciation. Now is the time to go live your real, not perfect, happy life.

I did it. My clients do it, too. They overcome the obstacles holding them back, and they heal, grow, and get on with living. Relationships are waiting for you, as well as jobs, adventure, joy, beauty, and so much more.

HOLLY'S HEALING TIP
Healing creates opportunity.

I have shared many difficult aspects of my life; those moments inform, but they don't define me as a victim, and they don't hold me back. There are amazing truths about my life, too. I got married, had a child, started my own business, sold essays, went viral, wrote books, and helped people. I love my friends and family. I have plans to travel to parts of the world I have yet to see. I dance and have celebrity crushes on men who play superheroes. I've been a guest on podcasts and co-led retreats. I enjoy gardening and love Halloween. I enjoy sunsets and travel, and I enjoy the smells of autumn — cool and crisp — to my favorite perfume, and even sushi. It would be easy to go on and on. Life is full of things to be grateful for, and I make sure I pay attention to those at least as much as anything bothering me.

Being grateful is grounding. I feel it also gives hope and perspective.

Celebrate all of the work you did to heal your self-worth and identity. Look in the mirror and smile at yourself, and let the accomplishment sink in until you own it. Place both hands over your heart, palms facing down, and take three breaths in and out. Send unconditional love to yourself and let it fill you up. Fully receive that which you deserve.

Thank you for trusting me and this process. Continue on the path to self-care and healing, and you will find that you will be more able than ever to go forth into the world and live, love, and be happy!

HOLLY'S HEALING HOMEWORK:

What words do you use to define yourself?

What will you do for yourself today?

Love yourself unconditionally.

Afterword

My intention with this book was to help you love yourself through change. I wanted you to be reminded of who you are and remember to put yourself first on the list instead of last.

There's a profound difference between wanting to make changes in your life and believing you are less-than. Healing and change are both aspects of a journey that we as humans come back to again and again.

This book was intended to meet you wherever you are in the process and be there as a guide when you reach new plateaus. You will see the words and receive healing at the place you're in at any given moment.

Of course, I'm here to help you, too. My intuitive abilities are a gift I want to share with you to help you move through what's bothering you and help you be the person you want to be. It's possible. Happiness is an option. Growing pains won't last forever, but being stuck can.

I believe in your bravery, and I see your divinity. You've got this.

For more information on Holly and how to schedule a one-on-one healing session, in person or virtual, please visit: www.hollyhughesintuitive.com.

Bonus

In writing this book, I woke up one morning and distinctly heard a meditation being dictated to me. I immediately picked up my journal and wrote down what I heard. It is designed to help you cope and stay healthy during the pandemic.

GUIDED COVID MEDITATION

I want you to sit quietly. You may become aware of the ambient sounds around you. The noise in the kitchen or the voices nearby. That's okay. Sounds cannot disconnect you from this healing.

Notice your breath. Is your breathing shallow or impatient? Draw breath into your body using your diaphragm. Take a long, deep inhale. Fill your lungs and relax your stomach for the count of six and exhale for the count of eight. Do this twice. If you have any difficulty taking long, slow deep breaths in, do not judge yourself. Meditation is a judgment-free space.

I want you to root down into the Earth. This planet has withstood time long past the point we can comprehend. Consider the earth holy ground, a place of growth and rebirth. It's a powerful star. It's the place you chose to manifest a lifetime.

Feel the earth come up to meet you and create a throne just for you. Notice what that throne is made of and how it supports you unconditionally. Look at it. What is your throne made of? Is it stone, steel, or floral?

Does it cascade with water or beam full of fairy light? Does it shimmer with jewels and crystals? There is no wrong way to see it. Get comfortable. The throne vibrates with the grounding energy of Mother Earth, Gaia. The grounding energy revitalizes your cells. You may experience the sensation on your skin or in your body. This is called healing energy.

Breathe it in. Let the hum from the earth sync with your own soul's vibration. Next, imagine an inverted triangle of light above you. One of the points connects to your crown chakra at the top of your head.

Let this portal connect you to your highest self. Imagine it pulling up all of the fear you've been feeling, like a vacuum. It will bring it out of your mind and body and into spirit, where the light of God can heal it.

This is no time for fear. It is a time for re-imagining a new age where an old, fear-based paradigm cannot exist.

Place both hands over your heart and breathe in peace. Feel all of the love the universe has for you — not because you're rich or famous or have millions of likes on social media, but because you are a beautiful soul, a child of light who has chosen to lift the vibration of the planet. Help it move past negativity. Fill the atmosphere and permeate the global consciousness with positive energy. See the triangle above you and feel it fill you with light. Every space that once held a lower vibration of fear is now full of unconditional love. Imagine a waterfall of infinite love streaming through and around you.

Take a deep breath in, past the panic or fear of not being able to breathe. The light never stifles a body or spirit. It illuminates and heals it. Move your hands into a comfortable position, facing up to receive.

When doubt creeps in, gently push it aside. Noise cannot stop healing. Take a deep breath in and let it out. Remember the throne you're seated upon. Know the earth is supporting you in receiving the healing vibration of light.

You may ask this healing to remain with you. You may ask that it come to you at night so you may rest. You may ask that it support you and free you of old fear because the darkness you feel is not yours. You are here to be the light that heals not only yourself, but you are an example of healing for the world. You are an example that proves how the vibration of fear and negativity won't win.

Think of yourself as a single, lit match in the darkest of rooms. Your one match strike can be seen from a long distance. You are a light of hope.

Inhale fully, and sigh out your exhale. Thank the earth, your spirit guides, angels, and God for creating this healing space. Imagine the triangle above you moving back to the space it came from. See your throne melt back into the planet. Know that this healing is exactly what you needed. With gratitude, end with "Amen."

Acknowledgments

I want to thank my husband, Russell Hughes, for supporting me in everything I do. I'm free to be as creative as I am because you see me and love me. I love you, Izzy, and can't wait to see how your light changes the world.

Thank you to my clients who trust me with the most intimate details of their life, vulnerable truths, hopes, and pains. You're the reason I put myself out there. I sincerely hope I help you feel better.

Thank you to my editor, Betsy Thorpe, for walking me through the book proposal and helping me shape the content of this book into something readable. You are patient, kind, and inspirational. Thank you to creative genius, editor, and friend, Lorin Oberweger, for assembling my thoughts into a concise title. And thank you to my copy editor, Beth Rodgers, for making this book shine. I'm so glad our paths crossed. Thank you, Melissa McCawley for making my cover sing and Ava Howard for the fantastic cover photo.

Here's to my writing community — the people who carried me through the journey of writing this book. Nicole Garcia, you're the magic to my muse, my personal confidante and support system. Shout out to generous and supportive friend and dance soul sister, Soraya Jones, for giving me permission to use her name to describe another. Love to my OGs, Monica Hoffman,

Kirstin Smith, and Jennifer Sellers who were once upon a time social media friends going through the writing trenches with me, and who became my friends. Thank you P2P16 ladies: Rachel Luckett, Tara Lundmark, Ellen McGinty, Casie Bazay, Carolyne Topdijan, Anne Stubert, Justine Manzano, Michelle Pike, Pam Van Dyke, Ally Overy, and Kalyn Josephson for the writing support and cheering for me on the good and bad days. Thank you, Rob Moniot, for always understanding. Thank you, Jamie Bechtold, Danielle Boucree, and Deb Grant for your lifelong friendship. There's nothing quite as rare as a constant friend who has been through the good and bad and continues to love throughout it all. Thank you to my friends at the Women's National Book Association, Kristen Knox, Jessica Daitch, and Carin Siegfried, for their input and tips.

Thank you to all of the healers who have touched my life. The ones who helped me explore my gifts, the ones who became friends, and the ones I admire. I'm able to do the work I do because you taught me how to control and master my abilities. Shout out to my teacher and healer, Rae Orion, who is both dazzling and generous.

Thank you, Mom, for your love, support, friendship and for listening to me on the days when the process of creating this book was overwhelming. Thanks, Dad, for your love and allowing me to be vulnerable about our story.

Thank you to the Binder community. You're a treasure trove of support and information. And here's to my readers. I hope my journey helps you along yours.

About the Author

Holly Raychelle Hughes is an award-winning author and intuitive healer living in North Carolina. She infuses her unique personal style, intuitive gifts, and emotional healing stories into all of her work. Holly is passionate about helping others find their happiness.

When she isn't working with clients, you will find her writing, creating and leading retreats, dancing, or preparing for Halloween.

HOLLY'S HEALING HOMEWORK

Use the next few pages to articulate your feelings in a safe space.

HOLLY'S HEALING HOMEWORK

HOLLY'S HEALING HOMEWORK

HOLLY'S HEALING HOMEWORK

HOLLY'S HEALING HOMEWORK

HOLLY'S HEALING HOMEWORK

Made in the USA
Columbia, SC
06 January 2022

53612485R00124